STREETS OF THE CITY

a history
by Judy Pulley

CAPITAL HISTORY

First published 2006
ISBN 185414 294 1

Published by Capital History
P.O. Box 250, Harrow, HA3 5ZH

Printed by Thomson Press
Lyon Road, Harrow, HA1 2AG

The junction of Fleet Street and Farringdon Street, today's Ludgate Circus, in the early nineteenth century.

Contents

Shaftesbury House, Aldersgate Street, early 19th century.

PHOTOGRAPHIC CREDITS

Photographs are from the Capital History collection except the following:

Guildhall Library, Corporation of London: 7 bottom, 10, 13, 21, 22/23, 26, 34, 35, 41, 48, 51, 52, 53, 56, 57, 67, 68, 70, 71, 74 top, 75, 76, 80, 84, 88.

London's Transport Museum: 17

Memories: 14, 15

Museum of London: 16, 45, 90.

INTRODUCTION

This book of City streets has not been written as a guide book or as a definitive history. My intention has been to re-create the 'past' of each street, recalling events, buildings and personalities which have been part of its story. I have included, where appropriate, those streets and alleys leading off the main thoroughfares. The story ends with World War Two though sometimes reference is made to more recent dates in order to put events in context, to establish location or to explain the fate of a pre-1940s building or institution.

Although, this is purely a City of London book, areas outside the City boundary are sometimes mentioned briefly. Buildings on the north side of Holborn are included as they were within the City until 1994 though due to boundary changes are now in London Borough of Camden.

Even though the City of London's history really begins with the foundation of the Roman city of Londinium in the 1st century AD, most of the layout of its streets dates from Saxon times when the City was resettled by King Alfred in the 800s. Since this period, lines of some streets have altered enormously while some still follow their ancient routes.

The Great Fire of London in 1666 swept away the medieval city and despite the dreams of Sir Christopher Wren to re-structure it with wide avenues and piazzas, rebuilding adhered to the old street layout. Only King Street, Queen Street and Princes Street were newly constructed. Some are creations of the 19th century, such as Gresham Street, Queen Victoria Street and the west part of Cannon Street. During the Blitz of World War Two, many streets were destroyed and lost forever, disappearing as new plans totally redesigned some areas of the Square Mile.

The accounts of many streets contain references to the Halls of Livery Companies which have been part of the City's history since the 12th century. Initially known as guilds, they regulated and governed all trades, trained apprentices and looked after the physical and spiritual needs of their members. Their name was eventually changed to Livery Companies after the distinctive uniform or livery worn by the Companies' masters. Their strict control over trades declined during the 17th and 18th centuries, though 107 companies, some formed in the last 10 years, still play an important role in today's City of London. They support education and training in related trades, endowing schools and awarding grants. They also used their substantial resources and funds to support charities and community projects.

ALDERSGATE STREET and ST MARTIN'S LE GRAND

A mid-Victorian view from Aldersgate Street, looking south, shows Robert Smirke's grand classical building of the General Letter Office built in 1829. Two stagecoaches are seen near the entrance, and in the distance is a pony and trap, the contemporary equivalent of the car. Newgate Meat Market was situated at the end of the street.

The city gate of Aldersgate which gives the street its name stood roughly where the church of St Botolph is situated today and, from the 1500s, the area north of it – Aldersgate Without – became home to the fine houses of noblemen and the aristocracy: the Earls of Westmorland, Duke Lauderdale, the Earls of Suffolk, and the mansion of the Petrie family which became a prison during the Civil War. The area was viewed as greatly desirable and when John Milton moved here in 1639 after his marriage to Mary Powell it was 'because there were few streets in London more free from noise'. In 1644, Inigo Jones designed a grand house just north of where the Museum of London stands today, originally for the Earl of Thanet. It later became the home of the Earls of Shaftesbury, was then converted into an inn, and finally in 1750 became the City Lying In (or maternity) Hospital, continuing its medical associations until demolition in 1882.

In 1657 it was said that *Aldersgate Street resembleth an Italian street more than any other in London, by reason of the spaciousness and uniformity of the buildings and the straightness thereof, with convenient distance of the other houses; on both sides whereof there are divers fair ones.* After the Great Fire destroyed his home in St Paul's Churchyard, the Bishop of London had a grand new residence built in this area outside the city walls, between Aldersgate Street and Bartholomew Close. It was destroyed by fire in 1768.

6

Between 1750 and 1836, No. 150 Aldersgate Street was the home to George Seddon and Company who became one of the largest and most successful companies of cabinet makers and upholsterers in Europe, employing as many as four hundred apprentices. The company made furniture for royalty and nobility, one of their most spectacular pieces being a painted satin-wood bureau and dressing table, also housing an organ, for Charles IV of Spain.

The large roundabout above which the Museum of London stands today is a product of the 1960s rebuild of the area and development of London Wall. In this part of Aldersgate Street, in 1728, John Wesley attended, 'very unwillingly' he writes in his journal, a Moravian meeting house. It was here, during a reading of Martin Luther's Preface to the Epistle to the Romans, Wesley records, 'I felt my heart strangely warmed', experiencing his conversion. Ten years later, his brother Charles's conversion took place in a house in nearby Little Britain. This narrow thoroughfare running west from Aldersgate Street, and just north of the Gate itself, is probably named after a 13th century landowner Robert de Bretoune. From the mid-1500s, it was an area occupied by booksellers and printers. In 1711, the Spectator was first published in Little Britain and the following year, at the age of three, Samuel Johnson was brought to London by his mother and lodged at the house of Nicholson the printer. The purpose of their visit was to try to obtain a cure for scrofula, a complaint with which young Samuel was afflicted. A condition of the lymph gland causing skin disease, it had been believed since the time of King Edward the Confessor in the 11th century that the touch of the monarch would provide a cure, and was known as 'The King's Evil'. It was also here that Dickens set the 'dismal little office' of Jaggers, the lawyer in Great Expectations.

Even the Aldersgate itself had literary connections as in the mid-1500s John Daye, the leading printer of the time, worked from premises above the gate. From here he published most famously Foxe's Book of Martyrs and was also one of the first publishers of music in England. All City gates were by this time, substantial stone buildings with rooms above which were used as both residences and as workplaces. The gateway was known in the 11th century as Ealdredsgate and may have been named after a Saxon noble Ealdred who earlier rebuilt the old Roman gate to the city. Through it, in 1603, rode King James I of England (James VI of Scotland) making his first entrance to the city as monarch. Rebuilt in 1617, the new gate incorporated a low relief of the king on horseback and depictions of the prophets Samuel and Jeremiah.

Above A 17th century engraving shows Aldersgate as rebuilt in 1617.

Business premises at No's 162–170 Aldersgate Street, 1883, which include Ben & Co, opticians and furriers Woolf and Hyman, and Rayner & Co, house and office furnishers. The buildings on the left are of a much earlier origin, probably 17th century.

As at several other city gates, a church dedicated to St Botolph, the patron saint of travellers, has stood at Aldersgate since 1135. After being partially destroyed in the Great Fire, the church was not rebuilt for 120 years until, in the 1780s, Nathaniel Wright designed a successor. The last burial in its churchyard was in 1833, and it was subsequently laid out as a garden. In 1887 to celebrate Queen Victoria's Golden Jubilee, the painter George Frederick Watts put forward plans to create a memorial cloister in the garden to commemorate 'heroic sacrifice', remembering those who had lost their lives trying to save others. Tales of heroism included those of Thomas Simpson who 'died of exhaustion after saving many lives from the breaking of ice at Highgate Ponds' in 1885 and Elizabeth Boxall aged 17 who died 'trying to save a child from a runaway horse in Bethnal Green' in 1888. Eventually completed in 1899 with 53 plaques (more were later added), today it survives as a unique testimonial to bravery. The garden is known as Postman's Park reflecting the fact that since the 1820s this area has been dominated by buildings connected with the postal services. Even nearby St Paul's Underground station was, until 1937, called Post Office.

A view of the Smirke's General Post Office (formerly known as the General Letter Office) in the early 20th century just before its demolition in 1911. Public conveniences are shown in the centre of the road and a cart with long ladders, possibly those of a lamplighter.

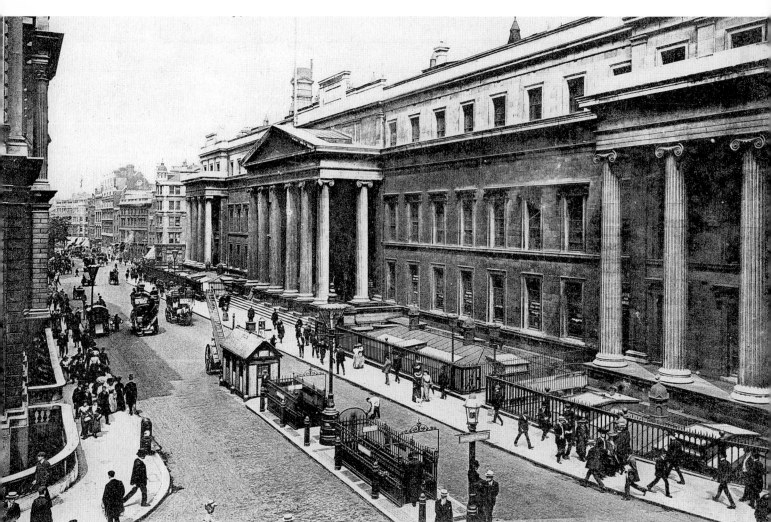

Just south of Postman's Park and north of Angel Street stands the building built in the 1890s as the General Letter Office. On this site since the 16th century had stood a large coaching inn, the Bull and Mouth. A small alley called Bull and Mouth Street led west opposite the end of Gresham Street (then called St Ann's Lane) and was the entrance to the inn. Its strange name was a corruption of Boulogne Mouth, commemorating King Henry VIII's siege of the mouth of Boulogne Harbour in 1544. The sign from the outside of the inn, depicting a large bull with a Cheshire cat-like grin, can be seen in the Museum of London. Angel Street is named after another inn, The Angel, situated just to south of the Bull and Mouth.

Postman's Park in 2005.

In the 1500s the house of the Percy family, the Dukes of Northumberland, was also situated here. The family later moved to a site in Northumberland Avenue off Trafalgar Square, and later still to Syon Park, Brentford, their main seat being Alnwick Castle.

South of the General Letter Office, Post Office buildings known as the West Range were built from 1869–73. This site is today occupied by BT, the former building being demolished in 1967. It was from there in 1896, that Guglielmo Marconi made the first public transmission of wireless signals. The most impressive of all the postal buildings in the street was the earliest. Opened in 1829 as the General Letter Office, this grand classical building with its entrance portico of Ionic columns was designed by Robert Smirke, architect of the British Museum and was very similar in style. This vast edifice stood at the southern end of the street in the part known as St Martin's le Grand, and on the east side. The building covered all of the area from Foster Lane to the east and St Ann's Lane (Gresham Street) to the north and was originally lit by a thousand gas burners. It was sadly demolished in 1911. The King Edward Building, completed in the same year, was constructed to replace it, on the west side of adjacent King Edward Street, and in 1927 under all of the Post Office buildings, a unique railway opened. It ran underground for six and a half miles, carrying mail from Paddington to Whitechapel via the main sorting office at Mount Pleasant but closed in 2003.

St Martin's le Grand was named after a monastery and college for priests founded here in the 11th century by brothers Ingelric and Girard. The college stood to the east of the present day road (where Smirke's Letter Office was later built) and to the west stood the precincts of the monastery. This area became a 'liberty' or sanctuary for those trying to escape the law, and was said to be the safest in England. Prisoners being transported from Newgate Prison to Tower Hill for execution sometimes managed to escape into its protection. The bells of the monastery sounded the city's curfew bell from the late-1200s for about 100 years. Those ignoring its sound were thrown into prison unless they were 'some great lord or other substantial person of reputation'. The tradition for ringing the curfew passed in the 14th century to four of the City churches – St Mary-le-Bow, Cheapside, St Bride's, Fleet Street, All Hallows Barking, by the Tower, and St Giles, Cripplegate. The City gates were locked at 9pm or dusk whichever came earlier and re-opened at sunrise or 6am whichever came later.

BISHOPSGATE and GRACECHURCH STREET

The south end of Bishopsgate in 1831 looking towards Gracechurch Street. The solid frontage of S. P. Cockerell's St Martin Outwich had only been completed 30 years earlier. Behind it is Nicholas Hawksmoor's tower of St Michael Cornhill from the 1720s.

At the point where Wormwood Street and Camomile Street cross Bishopsgate today is where the City Gate originally stood. Through it and north out of Londinium led the Roman road Ermine Street to Lincoln and York. Just outside the city boundary, the road passed a major Roman cemetery, just to the west of where Spitalfields Market stands today. The Gate itself, called Portam Episcopi in the Domesday Book, was restored and replaced several times until the 1700s, but unlike other City gates, it had no upper rooms in it, and was more of a triumphal arch.

An illustrated map of 1559 shows the land beyond the Gate as open pastures; cows are shown grazing in the fields, people walking and enjoying the country air and archers practising. The Gate itself displays executed heads.

Two priory hospitals were situated outside the City walls and along the line of the road. In 1197, on the site of the Roman cemetery, the Priory of St Mary Spital was founded, the land surrounding it becoming known as the Spitalfields. By the 1300s, the Priory gained a reputation for mismanagement and the bad behaviour of its canons, who became deep in debt. The custom of preaching a sermon at Easter from the Spital Cross in the churchyard continued after the Priory's closure. The Spital Sermon is still preached annually, though now in St Lawrence Jewry next to Guildhall, and is attended by the Lord Mayor.

The second priory was dedicated to St Mary of Bethlehem and founded by Simon Fitzmary in the 1240s. It covered the present site of the Great Eastern Hotel and Liverpool Street Station. Although at first the hospital cared for all types of illness, it became used from the 1300s especially for 'distracted patients' or the mentally ill. When the priory was closed down in the 1540s as part of the dissolution of the monasteries under King Henry VIII, the City Corporation took over responsibility for the asylum which became known as Bedlam, a corruption of 'Bethlehem'. It moved from here to London Wall in the 1670s. To the east of Bishopsgate were the practice grounds of the artillery through the 1500s and 1600s, until the Honorable Artillery Company moved to Moorfields in 1670.

During this period, a number of wealthy merchants and noblemen built houses in the area, several of which on the western side of the street still existed until the 1890s, when much of the area was demolished to make way for the expansion of Liverpool Street Station, which had opened in 1874. One was the house of Sir Paul Pindar, city merchant and for nine years, ambassador to Constantinople, who died in 1650. For about 100 years, prior to its demolition, his house had become a tavern and wine shop but luckily the high ornate timber façade was saved and is now in the Victoria and Albert Museum. Sir John Crosby's house, Crosby Hall, still exists in its entirety, as it was dismantled in 1910 and re-erected in Chelsea beside the Thames. The house was originally built in 1466 at the southern end of Bishopsgate, near to the church of St Helen's. In 1868 it became a restaurant and on its move to Chelsea was used by the British Federation of University Women. It is now once more a private residence.

Sir Paul Pindar's house.

Where Tower 42 (the former NatWest Tower) stands today, Sir Thomas Gresham entertained Queen Elizabeth I in January 1570. She dined here in his grand house on her way to open the first Royal Exchange, which it had been his inspiration to build and which he had personally financed (see CORNHILL). In the terms of his will, a college was to be established in his house. Named Gresham College, it provided free lectures on divinity, rhetoric, astronomy, music, law and geometry. Sir Christopher Wren lectured here and the house eventually became the first home of the Royal Society, Britain's foremost scientific institution founded in 1660. Robert Hooke, the first curator of experiments, lived in a courtyard apartment. The house was demolished in the late 1700s. Just outside the Gate in 1708, a workhouse was established for the poor of the city. 'Rogues, vagabonds and sturdy beggars' could be apprehended and set to work in it.

The principal entrance of the London Workhouse in Bishopsgate Street.

As Bishopsgate was a major route to the north, several coaching inns were situated here. Many were of the traditional design with timbered galleries surrounding a courtyard into which coaches pulled from the street, arriving from East Anglia and Cambridge. Here was the Black Bull, where plays were performed in the yard as was often the custom; the Catherine Wheel – its name remembered in Catherine Wheel Alley today; the Four Swans, the Green Dragon. The only inn still existing as a pub today is the White Hart at the corner of Liverpool Street, taking its name from the white deer emblem of King Richard II.

Dirty Dick's pub on the corner of Middlesex Street is named after Richard Nathaniel Bentley, owner of the pub in the 18th century, whose wife-to-be tragically died on the way to their wedding. He then locked up the room where the wedding breakfast was due to take place, which became dirtier and dustier as the years went by, and is said to have inspired Dicken's creation of Miss Haversham's room in Great Expectations.

To the east of Bishopsgate, the Cutler Street Warehouses were built in the 1760s to store the cargoes of the East India Company, unloaded from ships in the Pool of London and, after 1802, also from the new East India Dock. Buyers would come here to sample cargoes and to purchase. After the East India Docks' monopolies on tea and spices ran out, the St Katherine Dock Company took over these storehouses in the 1830s. They were then used by the Port of London Authority for over sixty years, from its creation in 1909. During the early 20th century, London became a major centre for the trade in eastern carpets, this being the last trade to leave the vast brick warehouses in the 1970s. One third of the buildings were subsequently demolished; the rest converted into offices including the oldest block, the Old Bengal Warehouse (1769–71).

Bishopsgate was once home to four churches, three of which survive today. St Ethelburga the Virgin, the smallest of all City churches and first mentioned in the 1250s, has been rebuilt after destruction in 1993 by a terrorist bomb, having survived the Great Fire and the Blitz in World War II. The church is dedicated to St Ethelburga, a 7th century Abbess of Barking, and its tiny façade is sandwiched between neighbouring buildings. In 1607, the explorer Henry Hudson and his crew of ten men and one boy took Holy Communion here before setting sail in their ship, the Half Moon, hoping to find a passage to the Orient by heading west. Hudson Bay and the Hudson River are named after him.

The church of St Martin Outwich once stood at the south corner of Threadneedle Street. The church dated from 1400 and was dedicated to Sir John Oteswich, its benefactor. It was apparently often referred to as St Martin at the Well with Two Buckets, which presumably stood nearby. Surviving the Great Fire, it was severely damaged in 1765 by a fire which began in an adjacent wig maker's and was demolished in 1794. Although a new church was then built, designed by S. P. Cockerell, in 1874, it was also knocked down to make way for Lloyds Bank which still stands on the site. All of the original church's fine Tudor monuments, including that of Sir John Oteswich, were moved to St Helen's Bishopsgate, one of the City's largest churches situated in Great St Helens just east of the main thoroughfare. St Helen's is particularly large as it has two parallel naves. One was the nave of the Benedictine nunnery established here in the 1200s and built against the nave of a parish church of even earlier origin, probably 1140s, though added to and embellished in the 14th, 17th and 19th centuries. No other part of the nunnery survives. Records show the nuns here were often being reprimanded by the Dean of St Paul's for their unacceptable behaviour – in the 1300s, for the number of small dogs kept by the prioress, for wearing 'ostentatious veils' and for 'kissing secular persons, a custom to which they have hitherto been too prone'. The prioress was ordered to keep the keys to the cloister gate 'for there is much coming and going out at unlawful times'.

St Botolph without Bishopsgate is just one of three City churches situated near City gates and dedicated to St Botolph, a patron saint of travellers. The 13th century church, where Sir Paul Pindar was buried, survived the Great Fire but was demolished in 1724. Sir Edward Alleyn, actor, theatre entrepreneur and founder of Dulwich College who died in 1560, was also buried in the old church. The present St Botolph's was built in the 1720s; Robert Hooke, scientist, architect and City Surveyor after the Great Fire was buried here and John Keats, the poet, baptised in 1795.

In 1865, the building which now stands on the north corner of Threadneedle Street was designed for the National Provincial Bank by architect John Gibson. At the time it was the most expensive building designed for banking use. He called the large central hall 'Gibson Hall', rather than naming it after the bank, as he hoped other City banks and companies would then hire it, which does in fact happen today though was less of a successful venture at the time. The National Provincial Bank was founded in Gloucester in 1834, and at first, only had branches outside London, which enabled it – like other provincial banks – to issue its own bank notes. This building heralded National Provincial's move to London. In the 1960s, a merger with Westminster Bank formed the National Westminster.

Bishopsgate in 1831 with St Botolph's church. The Watchhouse shown to the left of the garden was constructed in order to guard the churchyard against potential bodysnatchers. A similar building survives next to St Sepulchre's church in Giltspur Street. On the wall of the building on the left, a bishop's mitre marks the former position of the City gate.

Moving south towards London Bridge, Bishopsgate joins Gracechurch (formerly Grasschurch) Street, taking its name from the local hay and corn market. From Roman times, this was the main route into the City from the south leading to the forum and basilica (see LEADENHALL STREET). Consequently, in later centuries, it was where coaching inns grew up to serve the needs of travellers heading south into Kent and to the channel ports. In the 16th century, companies of actors began to perform in the yards of inns throughout London, and in 1594 the Lord Chamberlain's Men requested permission from Lord Mayor Martin 'to play this wintertime … at the Cross Keys in Gracechurch Street'. Perhaps they had previously upset the local residents, as the request states that 'they will now begin at two o'clock and have done between four and five, and will not use any drums or trumpets at all for the calling of people together, and shall be

Liverpool Street off Bishopsgate with Broad Street station (built 1865), now demolished. At the time this photograph was taken, Broad Street was the third busiest London railway station after Liverpool Street and Victoria. The short stone pillars on the right still exist today.

contributories to the poor of the parish'. Charles Dickens records, as a young man, watching the coaches at the Spread Eagle in Gracechurch Street.

The junction with Gracechurch Street, Lombard Street and Fenchurch Street was known in the Middle Ages as Carfax – a corruption of the French 'quatre voies' – 'four ways' – or crossroads. Junctions in the centre of some towns and cities today, such as Oxford, still bear this name.

Just to the south of the junction, stood St Benet Gracechurch where according to John Stow, a herb market was held opposite its west door. The church was demolished in 1867 for road widening. The pre-Fire church contained a monument to Queen Elizabeth I with a lavish inscription extolling the Queen's virtues – 'Britain's Blessing, Rome's Ruin, Netherlands' Relief, Heaven's Gem, Earth's Joy, World's Wonder, Nature's Chief'.

Bishopsgate looking north c. 1912. The Abercorn Rooms was the name given to the extension to the Great Eastern Hotel (on the left) completed in 1901. The elegant and ornate interiors include Hamilton Hall, the largest function room, decorated in Louis XV style and now a pub adjoining Liverpool Street station. The Duke of Abercorn was the father of the chairman of the Great Eastern Railway.

CANNON STREET

Cannon Street station in the 1930s in a photograph taken from the corner of Budge Row which then joined Cannon Street near to the junction of Walbrook and ran diagonally northwest. After World War Two, the line of Budge Row was changed. A Lyons Teashop stands on the corner with one of its delivery vans outside.

Cannon Street, as we know it today, has only existed since the 1850s. The street previously ran only from Gracechurch Street to Walbrook and then was extended to St Paul's Churchyard. It was constructed to follow a line of smaller streets and alleys – Apostle Lane, Little St Thomas Apostle, Basing Lane, Little Friday Street, Great Distaff Lane – whose names have now disappeared. Before this western section of Cannon Street existed, the main route to St Paul's ran along Budge Row and Watling Street slightly to the north, which still exist as minor thoroughfares today.

By the end of the 1st century AD, a street ran eastwards from Walbrook, through what seems to have been a prosperous part of the Roman city. Evidence has been found of grand town houses in the area, with tile roofs, mosaic floors and wall paintings. Most important is the vast building of over 42,000sq ft (13,000sq. m) that stood on the site of Cannon Street Station and under which some of it probably still lies. The scale of the building with its grand reception halls, living and administrative areas surrounding a courtyard with ornamental pool, suggests that this was the palace of the Roman governor of the Province of Britain. Travelling the country for most of the year as commander of the armies, Londinium would have been his winter base.

Outside Cannon Street station in March 1939. Most of the buildings of Cannon Street were soon to be destroyed in bombing raids.

Opposite the station, until World War II, stood the church of St Swithin London Stone, the only reminder of its existence now being St Swithin's Lane which ran beside it, leading to its churchyard. Built after the Great Fire, it unusually had no medieval predecessor and was considered to be a particularly masterful Wren church with a dome made up of eight segments. Formerly embedded in the church's wall and now in a 'cage' on the wall of the building facing Cannon Street is the block of limestone known as the London Stone. Its purpose and origins unknown, this mysterious object has been recorded since the 12th century and has variously been identified as a Roman milestone, funerary monument or part of the entrance to the governor's palace. In Shakespeare's Henry VI Part II the rebel leader Jack Cade strikes it with his sword, claiming, 'Now is Mortimer (his assumed name) lord of the City'.

From the 12th century onwards, Cannon Street's name is recorded variously as Candelwrithe Street, Canwickstrete, Candlewick Street – named for the makers of candles working in the area. The hall of the Tallow Chandlers Company has been situated in Dowgate Hill since the 1470s; some of the present hall dates from the 17th century. Candles for general household use were made of tallow whilst beeswax candles were for the church and nobility.

The area's other main industry was in fur, first traded in the area by the Hanseatic League (see THAMES STREET) in the 14th century. Budge Row dating from this time, takes its name from budgers who sold 'budge' or lambskin fur. The Worshipful Company of Skinners who traded in pelts and treated skins have been based on a large site in Dowgate Hill since 1409.

The streets from Queen Street, through Great St Thomas Apostle to Garlick Hill saw the main concentration of traders and auction rooms, some still trading until the 1980s. They ranged from small offices to the fur auction rooms of the Hudson Bay Company, founded in 1670 and for the subsequent 300 years the world's largest fur trading organisation. Despite their longevity, the company's first permanent saleroom was not established until 1928, when Beaver House, a Georgian style building, was built at the corner of Great Trinity Lane. The windows of the rooms where the pelts were graded faced north for the best light. Fur auctions, where two to three million pelts were sold, were held about ten times a year, lasting four to ten days. Replaced by the larger Hudson Bay House in the early 1980s, the auction house closed for business later in that decade.

To the west of Budge Row runs a small passageway, Tower Royal, where it is difficult to imagine the palatial house and tower that once stood here. Some evidence shows that a house existed from the reign of Henry I in the early 1100s, but by the 14th century it had become known as Tower Royal or the Queen's Wardrobe. The name 'Royal' comes not from a regal connection but is derived from the French wine producing region of Riole and referred to the vintners' trade which was based nearby (see THAMES STREET). However it was here that King Richard II's mother, Joan the Fair Maid of Kent, took refuge during the Peasants' Revolt in 1381. It was abandoned by the late 1500s, used for storage and stabling and destroyed in 1666.

Cannon Street suffered badly in the Great Fire as the flames spread rapidly westward from Pudding Lane. Late on the first day, 2nd September 1666, Samuel Pepys records in his diary that he walked east from St Paul's on his way home and *at last met my Lord Mayor in Cannon Street, like a man spent, with a handkerchief about his neck ... he cried, like a fainting woman, "Lord, what can I do? I am spent: people will not obey me. I have been pulling down houses, but the fire overtakes us faster than we can do it".*

Several churches were destroyed and never rebuilt: one on either side of the junction with Dowgate Hill – St John the Baptist to the west, and St Mary Bothaw to the east. A 'haw' was a yard where boats were built and repaired and it was in this church that Henry Fitzailwyn, the City's first mayor from 1189 to 1212, was buried.

After the Fire, despite Christopher Wren's dream to build the City to an entirely new street pattern, most was rebuilt to its old street plan. Queen Street, which cuts across Cannon Street from north to south, was one of the exceptions. Constructed as an approach to Guildhall from the river, it was named after Catherine of Braganza, wife of Charles II.

The streets off the western part of Cannon Street, as in other parts of the City, reflect past trades: Bread Street, Friday Street (a former fish market), Distaff Lane (where distaffs for holding wool and flax during spinning were made).

Before World War II, Cannon Street's prospect was largely a mixture of Victorian buildings influenced by Gothic or Classical styles. A large hotel, with a frontage of 230ft (70m) rose above Cannon Street Station. Inspired by French and Italian architecture and looking rather like Charing Cross today, it was designed in the 1860s by E M Barry, architect of the Royal Opera House and known as City Terminus Hotel. Here in 1920 the Communist Party of Great Britain was founded. The hotel closed in the 1930s and was subsequently used as offices.

Cannon Street was devastated in the bombing raids on the City. Virtually all of the buildings east of Bread Street were destroyed on 29th December 1940 – the worst night of the London Blitz. Two churches in Bread Street were lost: All Hallows, where John Milton was baptised in 1608, and St Mildred's, where Shelley and his second wife Mary Wollstonecraft Godwin (author of Frankenstein) were married after they eloped in 1816. Considering the destruction that occurred, it is therefore extraordinary that the tiny shop front at 115 Cannon Street survived and still stands today. Designed in 1936 by the eminent architects Walter Gropius and Maxwell Fry, it has glass bricks at the base and a facing of black Vitrolite glass, considered to be a luxury finish for shops at the time. It was built as the Mortimer Gall Electrical Centre, which sold electrical goods and light fittings.

The photo opposite shows Cannon Street in the late 19th century; this photo taken from a little further east shows the open space around St Paul's Cathedral created after the bombing of surrounding buildings in World War Two. Formerly hidden behind warehouses and offices, the tower of the church of St Augustine with St Faith survived after the rest of the church was destroyed.

CHEAPSIDE and POULTRY

An artist's impression of Old Cheapside. Timber-framed steeply gabled houses and inns line the wide thoroughfare, in this view showing Cheapside c. 1500. The larger monument on the left is the Eleanor Cross; the smaller is a fountain known as the Standard. The pre-Fire church of St Mary le Bow is seen at the foot of the picture. The countryside north and north-west of the city is seen in the distance.

Cheapside has the unique distinction of being the only street within the City of London that is narrower today than it would have been 500 years ago. As the main east–west route from the Tower to Westminster, it witnessed royal pageants of great splendour – joyous coronations when the buildings were adorned with tapestries and banners and the water conduits in the streets flowed with wine, heroes of battle returning from war, and sombre Royal funerals, such as that of Elizabeth of York in 1503 when a chronicler wrote 'Cheap was garnished with torches held by bearers in white gowns'. White was once the colour of mourning.

Geoffrey Chaucer in The Cook's Tale of Canterbury Tales (1300s) wrote of an apprentice who:

Whenever any pageant or procession
Came down Cheapside, goodbye to his profession.
He'd leap out of the shop to see the sight
And join the dance and not come back that night.

20

A view looking east towards Poultry c. 1780 with St Mary le Bow. All premises display sign boards advertising their wares. A line of posts protects pedestrians from carriages.

Until the 15th century, the area to the north of the street was a tournament ground for jousting. On one such occasion in 1330 to celebrate the birth of the Black Prince, the specially constructed stand on which Queen Philippa and her ladies were seated collapsed. Fortunately no-one suffered injury, and it was only the intervention of the Queen that saved the builders, as King Edward III wanted to execute them. In remembrance of this event, a small balcony overlooking Cheapside was incorporated into the design of St Mary le Bow church when Sir Christopher Wren re-designed it many centuries later. Builders working on the post-Fire church used the remains of a Roman road they had uncovered as foundations for the church's tower, explaining its position somewhat north of the 11th century crypt which still survives.

The first evidence of occupation in the area is in the area around Poultry, where the Romans established their first settlement in 47AD and later built a public bathhouse further west along Cheapside that was probably mainly for military use.

The busy west end of Cheapside at the corner of Old Change c. 1905 with buses and a Royal Mail coach to the right. The statue of Sir Robert Peel, founder of the Metropolitan Police and later Prime Minister was erected here in 1855. Removed in 1939, it now stands at the Police Training School in Hendon.

The western end of Cheapside before World War Two showing Nicholson's department store on the right.

The street's name – from the Old English 'ceap' or 'chepe' meaning 'to barter' – is indicative of its role probably from the Saxon period as the main commercial street in London, a position it held until the late 19th century. During the 1100s the street began to gain importance. The contemporaneous historian William Fitzstephen[1] writes that the area was full of 'men of trades, sellers of all sorts of wares, labourers in every work'. Still today the medieval street names off Cheapside remind us of how tradesmen gathered together in clusters: Bread Street, Milk Street, Wood Street, Ironmonger Lane, Honey Lane and Poultry itself where loriners also traded, manufacturing and selling metal sections of horse harnesses. Friday Street which today runs no further north than Cannon Street, then stretched as far as Cheapside. At the junction, until its demolition in the late 19th century, stood St Matthew, Friday Street, one of the smallest of Wren's churches, originating in the 1200s. Before the 1940s, Honey Lane ran fifty feet to the west of today's passageway of the same name and had been the pre-Fire location of All Hallows Honey Lane. From 1835, the City of London School was built here, having been founded in 1442, but due to rapid increases in pupil numbers moved to Victoria Embankment in the 1880s.

From the 12th to the 14th century, several small enclosed markets or 'selds' – rather like eastern bazaars – existed selling necessary commodities. However, by the 16th century, Cheapside began to gain a reputation for more luxurious goods and would have been lined with tall timber-framed buildings, often as much as five storeys high, with overhanging floors, high gables and chimneys.

The eastern end of the street was known as Goldsmiths Row, described in the 1560s as the 'beauty of London'. An indication of what was on offer here can be seen today in the Museum of London. Discovered by workmen in 1912, the Cheapside Hoard consists of 230 pieces of gold and enamelled jewellery, emeralds, amethysts and pearls – the wares of a local merchant, which were buried in a box in the early 1600s.

From the 1200s, Cheapside had been dominated by two large structures that stood in the roadway itself. At the eastern end was the Great Conduit, an ambitious scheme carrying water via lead pipes and cisterns from the Tyburn stream in the area of present day Oxford Street. The flow was not always reliable and although it was free to all, there were often disputes when tradesmen such as brewers tried to get more than their fair share. An underground stone chamber, forming part of the system, was found by archaeologists in 1994. Near the corner of Wood Street, an Eleanor Cross was erected in 1290 to mark the overnight resting place of the body of Eleanor of Castile, wife of King Edward I, on the journey from Northamptonshire to Westminster Abbey for burial. The enormous three-storey monument, decorated with statues of the Pope, Virgin and Child and Apostles, was finally demolished in 1643 'to cleanse that great street of superstition'. Small surviving pieces can be seen in the Museum of London.

The Great Fire destroyed the churches of St Peter Westcheap (also known as St Peter at the Cross on Cheap) which stood at the corner of Wood Street and St Michael-le-Querne, situated at the far west end of the street at the junction with Paternoster Row and named after a nearby corn market. Ralph Tresswell's survey of 1585 shows an illustration of the church with a water conduit outside

[1] William Fitzstephen was a cleric working for Thomas Becket, Fitzstephen wrote Becket's biography a few years after his death in 1170. He included as the preface 'A Description of London', the first recorded account of the City by a Londoner.

24

surrounded by buckets. The medieval church had only been rebuilt in the 1640s with Inigo Jones acting as consultant. Both Poultry churches were also lost: St Mary Colechurch and St Mildred, and although the latter was rebuilt, it was demolished in 1872.

Today the magnificent steeple of St Mary-le-Bow church punctuates the skyline, topped by a dragon weathervane almost three metres long. Rebuilt by Sir Christopher Wren after the Great Fire in 1666 had destroyed the medieval church, the steeple survived the enormous damage received by the rest of the building in World War II. It is the home of Bow Bells, within the sound of which you must be born in order to be a true Cockney. These famous sons of Cheapside can make that claim – Thomas à Becket (Ironmonger Lane, 1118); Sir Thomas More (Milk Street 1478); John Milton (Bread Street, 1608).

Cheapside in the early 20th century. None of these buildings survived World War Two except St Mary le Bow which was severely damaged.

From the 1390s, the Mercers' Company began to occupy the hall of the Hospital of St Thomas of Acre or Acon, which stood on the corner of Ironmonger Lane and had originally been established in 1227 to commemorate the site of Thomas à Becket's birthplace. Their business was the export of wool and the import of fine cloths such as linen, velvet and cloth of gold. After building a hall of their own nearby in the early 1400s, they bought the rest of the hospital's buildings including its church after the Dissolution. They are the only livery company today still to maintain a chapel within their premises, which now date from the mid-1950s. Now hidden from view from the main street in Ironmonger Lane, previous Mercers' Halls all had grand facades along the north side of Cheapside. The medieval hall had been destroyed in 1666. Samuel Pepys records in his Diary on 5th September how he picked up a piece of glass from the Mercers' Chapel 'so melted and buckled with the heat to be like parchment'.

Cheapside revived quickly after the Fire. A grand four-storey house built in 1668 for merchant Sir William Turner was not demolished until 1930, whilst at the corner of Wood Street, two small two-storey shops originally built in 1687 still stand as rare examples of their time. After the Fire, the Rebuilding Act of 1667 described four levels of building that were allowed to be built. Sir William Turner's house was at the highest level, while these properties, a shop with a room above and one below, were described as 'the least sort of building'. Now with 19th century frontages, the shops are still trading over 300 years later. By 1720, Cheapside is referred to as 'a spacious street adorned with lofty buildings, well inhabited by goldsmiths, linen drapers, haberdashers and other great dealers' and although beginning to lose its importance to Oxford Street as *the* shopping area, writers and travellers in the 19th century talk of the 'thronged street' and the 'dense mass of people'.

Today Cheapside's buildings are largely offices built since the destruction suffered in World War II, but it is still the main shopping street in the financial district. Before World War II, in Bird in Hand Court, on the south side of the street since 1870, stood Simpson's Fish Ordinary restaurant, where an 'ordinary' or everyday set three-course meal was served, the main course being fish. Grace was said before the meal and diners were invited to guess the weight of an enormous cheese on display. The prize for a correct guess was free champagne for everyone at the table.

CORNHILL

An engraving showing Cornhill
c. 1630. Part of Thomas Gresham's
original Royal Exchange with its tall
tower and arcades is shown as is the
circular building known as the Tun,
which had been a prison since 1200s
and where a water conduit was
established in the early 1400s.

The eastern end of Cornhill is the City of London's highest point – hardly a
hill today, but seen by the Roman founders of the City as an advantageous
position of defence, together with Ludgate Hill to the west.

The church of St Peter upon Cornhill, standing at the corner with Gracechurch
Street, is reputed to have been founded in the 2nd century AD when permission
was given for a Christian church to be built near to the Forum (see
LEADENHALL STREET). Close by, the church of St Michael, a Wren church with
a tower by Nicholas Hawksmoor, was founded in the 11th century. Very little of
Wren's church survives, as in the late 1850s it was transformed by George Gilbert
Scott who redesigned the porch, windows and much of the interior.

A medieval grain market was situated here giving Cornhill its name. Before the mid-1300s, it was the only market in England allowed to trade after noon. This however encouraged the practice of selling substandard goods under the cover of darkness, so after 1360, the market had to close at sunset. Earlier, in the 1100s, this district was a 'soke' or area that came under the particular jurisdiction of the Bishop of London, who could, among other things, compel all tenants to bake their bread in a public oven and charge them for the privilege.

In 1282, during the reign of Edward I, the Tun prison was established in the street, so named as it was said to be shaped like a tun or barrel. It was initially for those classified as 'night walkers' – those who disobeyed the curfew, and 'armed persons and those of a suspicious nature who walked the streets at night'. Bakers and millers who were caught stealing flour were also incarcerated and so were priests accused of becoming too 'familiar with female parishioners'. Nearby there was a pillory originally for traders involved in false dealing in the grain market, but still in use by 1702, when Daniel Defoe spent a day in it for issuing a famous satire 'The Shortest Way with the Dissenters'. He was later imprisoned in Newgate.

The maze of alleyways to the south of Cornhill – St Michael's Alley, Castle Court, Change Alley – retain the late 17th century character of this area when the coffee houses were established. They came to lay the foundations for many of the City's commodity markets, by providing places where merchants could meet to do business and establish contacts. The first coffee house in London was in St Michael's Alley in 1652 where, merchant Daniel Edwards set up his servant Pasqua Rosee in business, selling coffee at a penny a cup. Early advertisements sang the praises of this new beverage, which 'quickeneth the spirits making the heart lightsome'.

The popularity of the coffee houses led to a rapid rise in their numbers, each one becoming associated with different areas of interest. Examples were the Jerusalem at 32 Cornhill, where members of the East India Company met, and Jonathan's in Exchange Alley (now Change Alley) where speculators met in the early 1700s at the time of the rapid rise in value of shares of the South Sea Company, an event known as the South Sea Bubble. In 1760, 150 brokers formed a club here and thirteen years later, named themselves The Stock Exchange. Garroways, also in Exchange Alley, was associated with of 'men of learning and quality' and was a regular haunt of Sir Christopher Wren. Here, as in many coffee houses, auctions were held, known as 'sales by candle', the moment the candle died signalling when the last bid was accepted. Tea was auctioned at Garroways in this manner for the first time in England in the 1670s, fetching the enormous sum of £10 a pound (the equivalent of around £600 today).

In Castle Court, the 18th century George and Vulture Inn survives, described by Dickens in Pickwick Papers as 'good, old-fashioned and comfortable', and supposedly taking its name from a vicious parrot belonging to an early landlord. The parrot was nicknamed The Vulture by those customers unfortunate enough to be attacked.

After the Great Fire, some publishers and booksellers had drifted east from the area of St Paul's Churchyard which had been their traditional home. In the late 1600s, Thomas Guy, later to become the founder of Guy's Hospital, owned a bookshop selling bibles at the junction of Cornhill and Lombard Street. In the 1840s, at No. 65 Cornhill, were the offices of the publishers Smith & Elder to whom Anne and Charlotte Bronte sent their manuscripts, initially calling themselves Acton and Currer Bell, but later paying a visit to the publishers to reveal their true identities. Smith & Elder were also the publishers of William Makepeace Thackeray. In the 18th century, Cornhill had a reputation as a street of luxury goods – particularly linen drapers.

The 2nd post-Fire Royal Exchange which opened in 1671, shown in the late 1830s when its main entrance was on Cornhill. A cast iron pump which stood outside still stands today.

For almost five centuries, the western end of Cornhill has been dominated by the Royal Exchange. Until the present building was completed in 1844, the main entrance to the Exchange was on Cornhill itself. Thomas Gresham, originally from Norfolk and an agent of the Crown, who raised and negotiated loans abroad on the monarch's behalf, founded the first Exchange opened by Queen Elizabeth I in 1570. Based on the Bourse in Antwerp which had inspired Gresham, it was built on four sides around a courtyard with arcades of small shops known as 'the pawn' selling haberdashery, millinery, fancy goods, and also 'old and new armour'. The bell tower was topped with a golden grasshopper, the Gresham family crest.

Here in June 1583 the earliest surviving life assurance policy in England was drawn up, to insure the life of William Gibbons for the sum of £383 6s 8d; the policy to run for one year. When Gibbons died in May 1584 the underwriters involved insisted he had outlived the policy, counting 28 days per month rather than a calendar year, but were eventually forced to pay up.

Destroyed in the Great Fire, this building is described in Samuel Pepys's diary on the Fire's second day, Wednesday September 5th – 'The Exchange a sad sight, nothing standing there of all the pillars and statues'.

The second Exchange opened in 1669 and was divided into specific areas for the different nationalities and trading groups: the Irish Walk, East Country, Norway, East India, Virginia, Jamaica, Spanish, Jews, Turkey, Portugal, Scotch, Canary Walks; Clothiers, Silkmen, Salters, Grocers, Druggists, Brokers of Stock. Lloyds moved into the building in 1774 and remained a tenant until 1923, when they moved to their present site in Leadenhall Street.

In 1819, a new clock tower was added to the building. Fitted with a carillon of bells, it played a different tune each day – 104th Psalm on Sundays, 'God Save the King' on Mondays, and on Wednesdays 'There's Nae Luck Aboot the Hoose'. Quite by chance this tune rang out in January 1838 as the second Exchange burnt down. Arctic weather conditions meant that water from the pumps turned to ice on the ground. Queen Victoria and Prince Albert opened the present building in 1844, now realigned, with its entrance to the west.

A considerable area of Cornhill was destroyed in a fire in 1748, said to have been started by a servant who left a candle burning, though the street largely escaped damage in World War II. Today, due to the survival of many of its banks and offices of the late 19th and early 20th centuries, much of the character of a City street from this period still survives.

Cornhill looking west from the junction of Gracechurch Street.

The grandiose 1890s bank of Prescott, Dimsdale, Tugwell and Cave, now a stylish Cornhill pub.

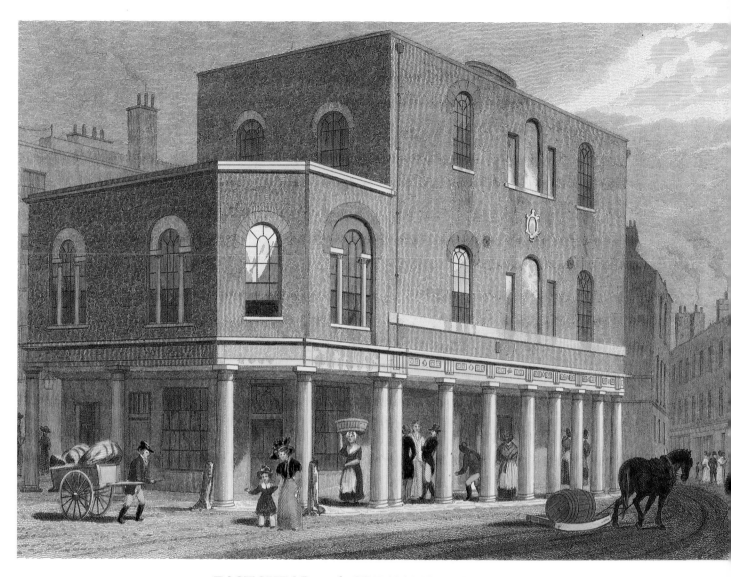

EASTCHEAP and GREAT TOWER STREET

The King's Weighhouse was established in the City by 1300 and was where imported goods could be officially weighed at the Great Beam. All goods above a certain weight that had entered port from overseas were supposed to be taken here so that the King could take excise on them. Moving to Eastcheap from Cornhill in 1666, it was closed down 30 years later, becoming a dissenters' chapel until the period of this engraving in the 1830s.

Prior to the construction of King William Street in the 1830s as a new approach to London Bridge, the street known as Eastcheap today was called Little Eastcheap, but there was another section of road to the west of Gracechurch Street. Known as Great Eastcheap, it stretched the short distance to Nicholas Lane. Today the church of St Clement Eastcheap standing in Clement Lane is nowhere near Eastcheap but it once was. East of Rood Lane, Great Tower Street (then called Tower Street) began as it does today, though its route to the east then ran along the south side of All Hallows Barking church. The street was first recorded as Tourstrate in the 1200s. In the 1880s, Eastcheap and Tower Street were widened to accommodate the extension of the Metropolitan District Railway beneath and Byward Street was created changing the line of the main east route to the north of the church.

Little Eastcheap, the City's eastern market area, had sold meat since the 1300s. John Stow[1] wrote *This Eastcheap is now a flesh market of Butchers there dwelling, on both sides of the streete, it has sometime also Cookes mixed among the Butchers and such other as sold victuals reddie dressed of all sorts.* Pudding Lane (also see THAMES STREET) takes its name from 'puddings' – intestines and entrails of the slaughtered animals – and was the site of the hall of the Worshipful Company of Butchers from the 1670s to the mid-1800s. The Bakers' Company have occupied a hall in Harp Lane, south of Great Tower Street, for 500 years.

At the western end of Eastcheap on the corner of Fish Street Hill, St Leonard's church was one of the first destroyed in 1666. Nearby, roughly on the site of Monument Station today, stood St Michael Crooked Lane, demolished in 1831 to make way for the new route of King William Street leading to London Bridge. Lord Mayor William Walworth financed many extensions to the church in the 14th century and was buried here after being fatally stabbed at Smithfield by Wat Tyler during the Peasants' Revolt. The first fatalities in the Great Plague of 1665 were recorded in the church. Before the new road construction, St Michael's Lane was parallel to and west of Fish Street Hill. Crooked Lane, well known for shops selling bird cages and fishing tackle, began here, ending at Pudding Lane.

The lanes running south off Eastcheap slope steeply towards Lower Thames Street as a reminder of how once the ground descended towards the banks of a much wider river. Today two churches are situated in this area: St Mary at Hill, damaged in the Great Fire, and St Dunstan's in the East, where a beautiful garden now lies within the shell of the walls left after bombing raids in 1941.

To the north of Eastcheap, St Margaret Pattens was possibly named after 'pattens' – wooden platforms worn to protect shoes from mud, which were made nearby. It is topped by a rare example of a timber spire clad in lead and was said to be one of Sir Christopher Wren's favourite designs. One of its unusual canopied pews bears the monogram CW 1686 though this may merely signify 'church-warden'. To the west of the church runs Rood Lane taking its name, according to John Stow, from a crucifix or rood which once stood in the churchyard. Beside its entrance is an early 18th century house, once the rectory. This is a rare survivor in the City, its classical shopfronts being added in the 1830s.

All Hallows Barking by the Tower at the east end of Tower Street reputedly had its origins in the 600s when it was founded by Barking Abbey in Essex, though remains uncovered after the destruction of the nave in World War II, are now thought to be 11th rather than 7th century in origin. Remains of the pavements of a Roman house, probably dating from the 3rd century, have also been found. William Penn, founder of the colony of Pennsylvania, was baptised here in 1644 and it was from the top of its tower that Samuel Pepys looked down on the City after the Great Fire, 'the saddest sight of desolation that I ever saw'. He had earlier commented on the desperate measures taken to stem the spread of the Fire, *Now begins the practice of blowing up of houses in Tower Street ... which at first did frighten people more than anything, but it stopped the fire where it was done ...* Pepys lived in Seething Lane which then ran past the church's west door and worked at the Navy Board offices on the east side of the lane which were eventually demolished in the 1780s. The site was then occupied by bonded warehouses

The Monument erected to commemorate the Great Fire of London viewed from the Eastcheap end of Fish Street Hill.

[1] A tailor by trade, John Stow walked the City, researched archives and chronicles, publishing in 1598 'A Survey of London'. He died in 1605 at the ripe old age of 80.

of the West and East India Dock companies. Their high brick walls contained the most extraordinary array of exotic goods – carved ivories, ambergris, cinnamon, nutmeg, cardamoms, dried turtle, everlasting flowers, durries, essential oils, feather fans, gongs, glue, peacock and osprey feathers, quinine, silk, shellac, sarsaparilla, sandalwood, verdigris, whalebone, vanilla. In the 1830s, the warehouses were sold off to various dock companies, surviving until the early 20th century. The grand building of the Port of London Authority which by then had taken over the running of the docks, took their place.

At the north end of Seething Lane stands St Olave's Church where Pepys worshipped and is buried. The street's name is said to derive from the Old English word 'sifethen' meaning full of chaff, perhaps referring to a nearby corn market. The first formal Corn Exchange was constructed between Seething Lane and Mark Lane in the 1740s, designed by George Dance the Elder. A second New Exchange was added to the Old Exchange in the 1820s, the original central open courtyards of which were covered in the 1850s by a metal and glass roof supported by iron girders. It was all rebuilt in the 1880s and traded not only in cereals but also in pulses, seeds, animal feedstuffs and fertilisers.

The Corn Exchange's 2nd building built in the 1830s and replaced in the 1880s.

The London Gazette in 1688 contained the first recorded reference to Lloyds of London at its first home in Tower Street. An advertisement asks for information following the theft of five watches from a man from Derby: *Whoever gives notice of them at Mr Edward Lloyd's coffee house in Tower Street, or to Mr Edward Bransby in Derby . . . shall have a guinea reward.* Virtually nothing is known about Edward Lloyd or what his first coffee house was like except that he gained a reputation for being able to supply his clientele of merchants and shipowners with reliable shipping news, the vital factor in establishing Lloyds as the recognised place for obtaining marine insurance. Lloyds remained in Tower Street for almost a hundred years, moving then to Lombard Street and in 1774 into the Royal Exchange.

During the 1800s numerous warehouses, offices and sales rooms were established along Eastcheap, as trading moved away from coffee houses. One of the first was Joseph Woods Sales Rooms (1812) on the east side of Mincing Lane, built in a Grecian style and specialising in cargoes such as tea and rubber. In 1860, it was replaced by the Commercial Sale Rooms consisting of 200 sample rooms and offices. In 1935, Plantation House was built to house numerous commodities markets, particularly tea and rubber, but also housed spice merchants, banks, dried fruit importers, sugar merchants, wine shippers, cocoa and coffee merchants. It was on a vast scale, almost filling the block formed by Great Tower Street, Mincing Lane, Rood Lane and Fenchurch Street, its interior likened to a grand hotel where a maze of corridors held not only salerooms and offices but teashops, tobacconists, restaurants and hairdressers. It was demolished in 2002. The rather curious name of Mincing Lane is thought to be derived from 'mynchenes' – an Anglo Saxon word for nuns.

Some warehouses of the 19th century still survive. On the east corner of Lovat Lane, Sir Henry Peek's tea warehouse is decorated with a low relief carving of a camel train whilst on the north side of Eastcheap, opposite Lovat Lane is an extraordinary neo-Gothic building from 1868, built as the London depot of Hill & Evans, vinegar makers of Worcester. High on its façade a carving of a boar's head serves as a reminder of the famous 16th century Boar's Head Tavern located, not on this site, but in Great Eastcheap. Mentioned by Shakespeare as being a favoured drinking place of Falstaff, it existed until 1831 when it was demolished as part of the scheme for rebuilding London Bridge. Just to the west of the Hill & Evans warehouse on the corner of Philpot Lane stands the warehouse that housed spice merchants Hunt & Crombie in 1862. Under the eaves nestle carved heads of dogs and pigs, whilst on the Philpot Lane side of the building at about head height, a small pair of carved mice with a piece of cheese are depicted, said to have been added by workmen whose lunch was being constantly stolen. In the early 1800s, Charles Henry Harrod first traded in Eastcheap as a tea merchant and grocery wholesaler. He went on in 1849 to found the Knightsbridge store.

The largest warehouse, eight storeys high, belonged to Ceylon tea importers Mazawattee Tea. Built in 1864, it stood to the east of All Hallows, obliterating the view of the Tower of London, and was considered such an eyesore that in 1933 it was purchased by the Tower Hill Improvement Scheme, which was intent on demolition when the lease ran out in 1948. The building however did not survive as long, being destroyed by bombing on 10th May 1941.

Looking east to Eastcheap from end of Cannon Street. The statue of King William IV was erected in 1844 when King William Street which runs off to the left, was cut through as a new approach to London Bridge. Moved in the 1930s, he now stands in Greenwich Park next to the Maritime Museum. The small cart in the centre of the picture is delivering ice.

FENCHURCH STREET and LOMBARD STREET

Fenchurch Street looking west in 1753 with Ironmongers' Hall built 1748 and said to be the most impressive livery company hall of the age. The company had occupied this site since the 1450s but relocated after this hall was destroyed in World War One.

According to John Stow a stream called the Langbourne ran near to the street, and the name therefore comes from the 'fen' or marshy land on its banks. However, no evidence of the stream's existence has ever been found, although this area of the City today is part of Langbourne Ward. The City is divided into 25 administrative wards, each represented by an alderman. The derivation may also be from 'faenum' or hay, from the local Gracechurch Street market.

Fenchurch Street and the eastern end of Lombard Street follow the line of a road of Roman origin, the principal west-east road south of the Forum which eventually continued out of the City eastwards towards Camulodunum (Colchester), originally the capital of Roman Britannia. The road led out through Aldgate at the eastern end of the street. Before 1600, Aldgate was apparently in such a state of neglect and disrepair that the phrase 'as old as Aldgate' was a commonly used phrase within the City. The origin of the name, however, is thought to have been the 'old gate' – the Saxon '*Ealdgate*'. From 1374 to 1385, the room above the gate was leased to the poet Geoffrey Chaucer, then comptroller at the nearby Custom House. On the accession of King James I in 1603, the gate was rebuilt. On its east façade, facing out of the City, there were statues of two men in armour holding great stones, as if about to drop them on any enemies advancing on London. The gate was demolished in the 1760s.

34

There were once four churches in and near Fenchurch Street, none of which survive. Unusually, St Gabriel le Fen stood in the middle of the road, and was originally referred to as St Mary's in the early 1300s. The reason for its name change is unknown. It was lost in the Great Fire as was St Dionis Backchurch, which stood on the corner of Lime Street. Dionis is a corruption of Denys, the French patron saint; Backchurch probably because it stood back from the street frontage behind a row of houses and shops. On Christmas Day 1664, Samuel Pepys recorded in his diary a visit here, remarking, 'a very great store of fine women there is in that church, more than I know anywhere else'. Unlike St Gabriel, St Dionis was rebuilt by Sir Christopher Wren, on such an irregular medieval site that it had no right angled corners to its main walls. In 1878 it was demolished, as many Wren churches were during the late 19th century, due to redevelopment and road-widening schemes. St Katherine Coleman, situated on the south side of the street near Fenchurch Street station, survived a little longer, being demolished in 1926. John Stow wrote of a nearby garden, Coleman Haw, probably named after a local benefactor and the original builder of the church. St Katherine's had escaped damage in 1666, but had then been rebuilt by James Horne in the Palladian style in the 1730s.

Aldgate, demolished in the 1760s along with the other City gates.

On the west side of Mark Lane, the 15th century tower of All Hallows Staining is all that remains of a church demolished in 1870. Its name derivation is unknown but it may be that the land once belonged to the manor of Staines. Here in May 1554 Princess Elizabeth, later Queen Elizabeth I, is said to have given thanks after her release from the Tower of London, and given new bell ropes to the church as the sound of the bells had so delighted her. She had been imprisoned following a suspected implication in the Wyatt Rebellion against her half-sister, Mary Tudor. On the other corner of Mark Lane stood the King's Head Tavern where she supposedly went on to a supper of pork and peas, the pub then being renamed The Queen's Head.

The inn at the sign of the Elephant, 120 Fenchurch Street, where a tavern had stood since before the Great Fire and where a pub called the Elephant still exists. The painter William Hogarth is said to have lodged at this address.

The Elephant Tavern at No. 120 is today identified by a splendid elephant sign hanging outside its modern premises. There has been an inn here of the same name since before the Great Fire. The old premises were rebuilt in 1826, and then bombed in World War II.

Next door stood the Ironmongers Hall from the company's foundation in the 1450s. As well as producing basic iron goods such as horseshoes and cartwheels, they also supplied iron cressets, open ironwork baskets in which wood and coal burned that were carried by men of the Ironmongers Company in the great medieval torchlit processions. By the 1740s, they occupied a classical style building round a courtyard which was one of the few bombed in World War I. After its demolition in 1917, the company moved to their present home near the Museum of London.

The Clothworkers Company still occupies the site on the corner of Mincing Lane and has done so since 1472. Prior to this, the Shearmen's Hall was situated here until they, and several other craftsmen such as the Fullers, merged to form the Clothworkers in the 1500s. Samuel Pepys was the master of the company in the 1670s.

St Dionis Backchurch, corner of Lime Street and Fenchurch Street, in 1830. The fact that the church is set back from the street behind shops is probably why it acquired this name. Following demolition of the church in 1878, the 18th century organ was acquired by the Merchant Taylors' Company for their Threadneedle Street hall.

Connections with the river and London's earlier port are never far away in this part of the City. On the late 19th century building at No. 153 is a trade sign of Tull & Co, rope and twine makers, made in terracotta bricks dating from 1700s. It depicts two men in a boat (of a particular type known as a peterboat) beneath a carving of a doublet. Tull & Company traded at the sign of the 'Peterboat and Doublet' at a time when, before the numbering of premises, all business were identified by a pictorial sign.

At the opposite, eastern end, of Fenchurch Street stands Lloyds Register of British and Foreign Shipping, founded in 1760 and located here since 1901, occupying a wonderfully ornate building. Lloyds Register compile a complete list of all ships in the world over 100 tons, laying down standards to which they must conform and categorising them, the highest ranking being A1.

Shipping merchants in the 19th century were not permitted to go to the docks to inspect cargoes. The West India Dock Company had offices in Billiter Square where samples could be viewed and checked. Billiter Square and Street were originally 'Belseterslane' in the 1290s, where bellfounders worked. They were constantly in demand. The City then had over one hundred churches whose bells rang out not only for special occasions, but marked the daily hours, the times of every service and devotion and often the curfew – a medieval citizen's life was governed by their sound.

The daily 'commute' for thousands of workers into the Square Mile really began in 1841 with the opening of the City's first railway terminus in Fenchurch Street for the London & Blackwall Railway. No further City railway stations were built for twenty years, until Blackfriars and the now closed Broad Street followed in the 1860s.

From as early as the 14th century, Lombard Street came to symbolise more than any other street in the City, the world of banking and money-lending and is where two major clearing banks were situated for almost three hundred years.

It took its name from Lombardy when, after the expulsion of Jewish financiers by Edward I in 1290, Italian goldsmiths took their place and settled in this area of the city. From their language, words such as bank (from the Italian 'banco' meaning desk), debit and credit originate. Banks began to develop from the goldsmiths' trade during the 17th century when, after accepting money for safe deposit, they gave a receipt in exchange. These could eventually be used as payment to a third party, thus becoming the forerunner of cheques.

Before the advent of street numbering systems in the mid-1700s, banks, shops and tradesmen were located by pictorial signs hanging outside their premises. Examples depicting a Cat and Fiddle, King's Head and Crown, a Castle and an Anchor decorate Lombard Street today acting as a reminder of former times although they date only from 1902 when they were erected to celebrate the coronation of King Edward VII.

In the 1720s, John Freames, a goldsmith, was trading at the eastern end of Lombard Street at the 'sign of the black spread-eagle'. On the marriage of his daughter, his new son-in-law joined him in business and eventually gave his name to the bank – Barclay & Company, who still have the eagle as their company logo today and continuously occupied the same site until 2005.

A view along Lombard Street to the east c. 1830. The church of St Edmund the Martyr is on the left and in the distance is the steeple of the now lost church of St Benet Gracechurch Street, demolished in 1867.

Most banks' histories involve complex amalgamations of many different companies and partners. Lloyds Bank is no exception and can trace its London origins to John Bland, another goldsmith, and contemporary of John Freames, trading at 53 Lombard Street at the 'sign of the black horse'. Lloyds Bank however did not adopt this as their symbol until the late 19th century when the Lloyds Banking Company of Birmingham took over the London operation by then known as Barnett Hoares Hanbury and Lloyd. They were the first bank in the City of London to install electricity in 1887 and, like Barclays, have only recently moved their head office away from Lombard Street.

Today most of Lombard Street's buildings post-date 1920 and its grand 19th century banks have not survived. They were mostly Italian Renaissance in style except for the imposing Gothic Clydesdale Bank designed in 1866 by Alfred Waterhouse (architect of the Natural History Museum) which stood at No. 32 but was demolished in the 1960s.

When King William Street was created in the 1830s, the angle of the western end of Lombard Street was altered and the powerful façade of St Mary Woolnoth, built by Nicholas Hawksmoor between 1716–27, was thus made more visible. In 1897 bodies from the vaults were removed to Ilford to enable a booking hall for Bank station to be created in the crypt.

The post-Fire church of St Edmund King and Martyr, further along the street, is unusually built on a north-south alignment and dedicated to Edmund, king of East Anglia, defeated and killed by the Danes in 870AD.

In 1938, Lombard Street's third church, All Hallows, was demolished to allow for the expansion of Barclays Bank. It had been almost completely hidden between other buildings and was known as 'The Church Invisible'. Its tower was rebuilt at All Hallows, Twickenham and many of its fittings reused.

Fleet Street in 1800 looking west to Temple Bar in the distance. St Dunstan-in-the-West is shown in the centre with the statue of Queen Elizabeth I which was removed from Ludgate in 1760, on the exterior wall. This church was demolished in 1830 in order to widen the street; a new church was built in line with the shops to the right.

FLEET STREET

Fleet Street, taking its name from the Fleet River, which ran at right angles to it at its eastern end (see LUDGATE HILL), is first mentioned in 1002, and by the late 1100s, William Fitzstephen describes the 'spacious and beautiful gardens' of the area just outside the City walls.

The association between Fleet Street and printing began in 1491, when Wynkyn de Worde, a pupil of William Caxton and successor on his death, re-located his presses from Westminster to a site near St Bride's Church. The area was ideal for business. Along this main route from the City to Westminster stood the town houses of bishops and abbots: to the north, Peterborough, Cirencester, and Winchcombe, to the south, Salisbury, St David's, and Faversham. Some street names today reflect their existence: Peterborough Court, Salisbury Court, and Poppins Court, after the popinjay or parrot, the Abbot of Cirencester's emblem.

Further east were the Inner Temple and Middle Temple, the habitats of lawyers since the 1300s. Trading at the sign of the Sun, de Worde made innovative changes to the world of print, including the use of italics, and produced hundreds of books, including an early work on the art of chess.

Although London's first daily newspaper, the *Daily Courant* was produced nearby in 1702, Fleet Street did not really become a street of newspapers until the 19th century. In 1822, the *Sunday Times* was first edited in Salisbury Court and by the end of the century, the eastern end of the street and area to the south were dominated by the printing works of the large national daily newspapers and offices of provincial ones.

The *Daily Telegraph* was founded in 1855, moving here in 1860; the *Daily Mail* founded by the Harmsworth brothers in 1896, cost a halfpenny and began a new style of popular press. This period also saw the establishment of the Press Association – to funnel national news, Reuters – collating international news and the Press Club. During the 1940s and 1950s, it was possible to take a tour to see the papers produced; for dailies such as the *Daily Mail* and *News Chronicle*, these tours were at 9.30pm, in order to see the next day's editions roll off the presses. The last newspaper to leave Fleet Street – the *Daily Express* – moved in 1989, but its black glass Art Deco building from 1930–33 survives at the eastern end of the street as does the old *Daily Telegraph* building from 1928–31, incorporating Egyptian and Greek influences in its design.

The clock of the former Daily Telegraph building.

To the east of the Express building, and forming the corner of Ludgate Circus stands the grand block built in 1873 as the London headquarters of travel company Thomas Cook. Carved stone heads representing different nations adorn the exterior. Previously occupying smaller premises on the opposite side of the street that included a boarding house, Thomas Cook had first come to London in the 1860s, and by 1873 was offering guided tours of the United States and most of Europe. A world tour at the time took about nine months. Turn of the century advertisements outside the building announced 'Saloon and Emigrant Tickets' and 'See the World By Steam'. The company moved its main office from here in 1923.

On the banks of the Fleet River, and to the south of Fleet Street, Henry VIII's Bridewell palace was built in the 1520s. Its brick buildings surrounded two inner courtyards and it took its name from a nearby holy well dedicated to St Bride, and from the adjacent church of the same name. The palace was probably the setting for the last meeting between Catherine of Aragon and the King prior to their divorce, and after 1531 was leased to the French Ambassador. Hans Holbein's painting 'The Ambassadors', now in the National Gallery, was painted here in 1553. Later that year the palace ceased to be a grand residence when King Edward VI gave it to the City to be used as a short term prison for vagrants, petty offenders, 'disorderly' women and as a home for destitute children. Its use as a prison continued until closure in 1855.

The church of St Bride is perhaps the earliest place of Christian worship in London, as World War II damage led to the discovery in the crypt of a Roman pavement which could have been part of a church from that period. There is evidence of the existence of six churches prior to Wren's post-Fire church of 1675, the first recorded dating from the 6th century. Its dedication is to the Irish saint St Bridget or St Bride, her popularity perhaps arising from the rumour that she could turn water into beer. The parents of Virginia Dare, the first English child born in colonial America (1587) were married here, as were those of Edward Wilmslow, one of the leaders of the Pilgrim Fathers.

Samuel Pepys, born in neighbouring Salisbury Court, was baptised in St Bride's Church in 1633, together with his eight brothers and sisters. Just before his birth, the Salisbury Court Theatre opened in the street where his family lived, and although officially closed in 1642, as all theatres were at the outbreak of the Civil War, it continued to hold clandestine performances. It re-opened in 1660 but burnt in 1666. In 1722, Samuel Richardson, often called The Father of the English Novel, began his printing business in Salisbury Court. His first novel, Pamela, written in 1740 at the age of fifty, warned of what may befall young women in domestic service in 18th century London and was published in monthly instalments. His second novel, Clarissa, followed seven years later and was twice as long as Tolstoy's War and Peace, with one million words. Dr Samuel Johnson wrote 'If you were to read him for the story, your impatience would be so great you would hang yourself.'

Further west from Salisbury Court lies Whitefriars Street, which before 1844 was known as Water Street, but then renamed after the Whitefriars or Carmelites who established a priory here in the 13th century. Their founder, Richard of Cornwall, brother of King Henry III, brought a group of monks who had been based at Mount Carmel, back from the Holy Land. Initially they were hermits living in remote areas of England, but were eventually allowed to base themselves in London to administer to the sick and poor. Tradition has it that the body of King Henry VI was taken here after his murder in the Tower in 1471, prior to burial in Chertsey Abbey, his body eventually being moved to Windsor. After the Dissolution, the priory's refectory became the Whitefriars Playhouse, used by children's companies such as St Paul's Choristers and the Children of the Queen's Revels.

As at all medieval religious houses, an area of sanctuary existed around Whitefriars for those escaping the law who could reach its precincts. Although abolished elsewhere after the Reformation, this right could still be claimed here and the area became a gathering place for villains and thieves – a no-go area known as Alsace or Alsatia after the then lawless territory between France and Germany. The area and its inhabitants remained outside the law until 1697 when the privilege was finally abolished.

There are records of a small glass factory in this area between Fleet Street and the river in the early 1700s – the beginnings of world renowned Whitefriars Glass which continued production here until 1923. Responsible for such diverse products as chandeliers in the 18th century and stained glass designed by Burne Jones and Rosetti in the 19th, when the factory moved to Wealdstone, Middlesex, a brazier was lit from the old furnaces and taken to re-ignite the new. From 1690 to 1713, on the corner of Whitefriars Street, stood the workshop of Thomas Tompion known as the father of English watchmaking, who was clockmaker to the Royal Observatory in Greenwich and the first maker to produce a watch with a balance spring.

Shops on the east side of St Dunstan-in-the-West in 1883. The central premises specialises in music books while the fish shop to the right advertises cod, turbot and various types of oysters from a shilling to two shillings and sixpence a dozen.

Many buildings along the street have tall narrow facades, having been constructed on deep narrow plots, a consequence of medieval land ownership. Fleet Street itself was once extremely narrow especially at the eastern end, but in 1897 much of the south side was demolished to enable widening of the thoroughfare to a uniform 60ft (18m).

In early centuries, there was hardly any development to the north of Fleet Street and therefore very few streets of any size run off it in this direction but mainly narrow alleys and courts. Opposite Whitefriars Street and beside one of the City's oldest pubs, Ye Olde Cheshire Cheese, runs Wine Office Court where licences for the selling of wine were bought before 1666. Through the 18th and 19th centuries, the Cheshire Cheese was renowned for its huge savoury pudding full of steak, kidney, larks mushrooms and oysters. The buildings of the pub were originally two houses built just after the Great Fire, though the back of the pub facing Wine Office Court is 18th century. Two other Fleet Street pubs also date from the late 1600s, though superficially they appear to be much later. The Tipperary opposite the Cheshire Cheese has an 1895 interior inside a 1678 building, the Old Bell nearer to St Bride's dating from 1669 but with an 1897 façade. So numerous were the drinking establishments lining the street that in the 1700s a contemporary ballad refers to 'that tipling street'.

A view from Chancery Lane of the corner of Fleet Street in 1798 showing what are described as 'ancient houses' probably 16th century in origin. To the left, Inner Temple Gateway (1611) can be seen, at this time occupied by a waxworks.

A little further to the west, Bolt Court, probably named after a nearby coaching inn, the Bolt in Tun, leads to Gough Square where Dr Samuel Johnson lived at No. 17 from 1748 to 1759 and in the attic produced his most famous work, the 'Dictionary of the English Language'. Johnson lived in and around Fleet Street for most of his life, frequenting its taverns with literary friends such as Oliver Goldsmith and James Boswell. He died at a house in Bolt Court in 1784. In 1837 a Romanesque style church, Holy Trinity, was built on the northeast corner of Gough Square in a poor area with no place of worship, but was demolished in 1905. It was designed by John Shaw Junior, who collaborated with his father on St Dunstan's in the West. Crane Court was rebuilt after the Fire by speculative and often disreputable developer Nicholas Barbon, responsible for much rebuilding at this time. No's 5 and 6 survive. From 1710 to 1780, the Royal Society met in Crane Court with Isaac Newton as its first president. Founded in the 1660s, it is Britain's oldest scientific society. Newton petitioned for a lamp to be placed at the entrance to the alley to encourage people to enter. The magazines *Punch* and *The Illustrated London News* were both first published in Crane Court in the 1840s.

Only two early churches existed in and around Fleet Street. St Dunstan-in-the-West, however, is younger than St Bride's by at least 600 years, being first recorded in 1170. The old church stood 30ft (10m) further to the south making the street incredibly narrow and congested at this point. In order to widen the road, it was demolished and rebuilt in the 1830s by John Shaw Snr. Its magnificent clock dates from 1671, and was rescued from destruction. The statue of Queen Elizabeth I (1586) on the exterior and of King Lud and his sons in the porch were from Ludgate (see LUDGATE HILL). John Donne and William Tyndale both preached here.

Three important banks were established at this western end of the street in the 17th century. Hoare's Bank, opposite St Dunstan's, was founded as a goldsmith in 1672 at the sign of the Golden Bottle, but moved here and became a bank in 1690. Amongst their early customers were Samuel Pepys and John Evelyn, whilst later account holders included Thomas Chippendale, Thomas Gainsborough and Jane Austen. Until 1939 the 'running cashiers' or messengers wore knee breeches with silk stockings. Under the present bank (1829) parts of the cellars of the Mitre Tavern still exist. Dating from 1603 but demolished in the 1820s, it was one of Samuel Johnson's favourite haunts.

A little further west stood Goslings Bank, opened in 1684 and trading at the Sign of the Three Squirrels. Between the two today stands the late 19th century Cock Tavern; the original tavern was a favourite of Samuel Pepys but then stood opposite, on the north side of Fleet Street.

Child's Bank, the last building on the south side within the City boundary, and London's oldest bank, was founded in 1673 at the Sign of the Marigold. Accounts were held here by Oliver Cromwell, King Charles II and many of his mistresses including Nell Gwyn also by King William III and Queen Mary, and the first Duke of Marlborough. The bank appears in Dickens' Tale of Two Cities but is called Tellson's. Like Hoare's Bank, part of the Child's building stands on the site of an infamous drinking establishment. The Devil's Tavern was a favourite of dramatist Ben Jonson, who founded here the literary Apollo Club for intellectuals and committed drinkers in the early 1600s. The tavern's original name was the Devil and St Dunstan, with a sign depicting the incident where St Dunstan supposedly tweaked the Devil's nose with a pair of iron tongs. Almost next door, perhaps at No. 15, stood Nando's Coffee House, favourite with lawyers for a hundred years from the 1690s.

At the time of the creation of the Apollo Club, most of Fleet Street's houses and taverns would have been gabled and timber-framed but only one survives, Inner Temple Gateway (1611). Above the gateway Prince Henry's Room boasts a fine Jacobean plaster ceiling and is probably so-called because the building once housed a pub, The Prince's Arms, rather than from having a more definite royal connection. Some mythical tales grew up about the site and in the 1890s, Carter's Haircutting Salon who occupied the building advertised its business premises as being 'Formerly The Palace of Henry VIII and Cardinal Wolsey'. It was a waxworks in the early 1800s owned by a Mrs Salmon. Two similar houses existed on the other side of the road near to St Dunstan's until 1893.

Opposite the Gateway, Chancery Lane runs north to Holborn. First known as New Street, it was here in the 1200s that King Henry III set up a house for Jews willing to convert to Christianity. The Jewish community was expelled following an edict of King Edward I in 1290 and by 1377, the buildings were

A congested Fleet Street in 1905 with buses, private carriages and delivery vehicles. The bridge taking the railway across Ludgate Hill can be seen in the distance. To the right are the offices of the Daily Chronicle newspaper which began in 1872, merging with the Daily News to form the News Chronicle in 1930.

used by the Keeper of the Rolls of Chancery (official documents and records kept on scrolls of parchment). In the 1860s, the elaborate Gothic-style Public Records Office was built on the site and the ancient Rolls Chapel demolished.

To the south of Fleet Street is the area of Inner Temple and Middle Temple, land acquired by the Knights Templars in about 1160. Having built the originally circular Temple Church in 1185, they continued to occupy the land until their suppression in 1312. The Knights of the Order of St John then acquired the land, leasing it to lawyers and thus beginning the legal traditions of the area and leading to the establishment of connected institutions in and around Fleet Street. Sergeants' Inn, one of several in London, stood opposite Crane Court and was the residence for Sergeants at Law, who were senior barristers, from the 1400s until the 1700s. Both Sergeants', and Clifford's Inn, a little further west, established in the early 1300s, were Inns of Chancery (see HOLBORN). After the Great Fire, disputes over land ownership, property and tenancy rights were heard here at Clifford's Inn by 22 specially appointed Fire Judges. To the east of Clifford's Inn Passage stood Praed's Bank, designed by John Soane in 1801 but demolished in 1923.

Fetter Lane may take its name from 'faitor', Old French for a lawyer, and is first so-called in 1292. By the 14th century, the reputation of lawyers had sunk so low that 'faitour' had become a common insult for someone who was an idler or imposter. In the 1600s, Fetter Lane was known for its conventicles – illegal or secret religious meetings of dissenters, a tradition which continued into the 1700s with John Wesley and George Whitfield both preaching here.

The western boundary of the City of London, Temple Bar, is today defined by a granite memorial from 1888, decorated with statues and bronze reliefs,

surmounted by a City dragon. A barrier was first mentioned here in the 1290s outside the City walls yet marking an area still within City jurisdiction, the City Liberties. Originally probably consisting of wooden posts and a chain, by 1351 a large timber gate with a central arch had been built with a prison above. For the next five hundred years, accounts tell of great events passing under Temple Bar. The Black Prince, after victory at Poitiers in 1356 rode through with his captive, the King of France. For the wedding of Henry VIII and Anne Boleyn, it was 'newly painted and repaired' and, on the defeat of the Spanish Armada in 1588, Queen Elizabeth I was carried through on her way to a thanksgiving service in Old St Paul's Cathedral. It was perhaps on this occasion when the tradition of the Temple Bar Ceremony began. Each time the monarch enters the City, a stop is made here and permission asked of the Lord Mayor to continue within the City boundary. This is rarely required of the monarch today.

Despite the protestations of the Lord Mayor that the City could not afford it, King Charles II insisted that Temple Bar be rebuilt in 1669, even though the old arch survived the Fire. The grand new construction of Portland stone with royal statues on both sides was designed by Sir Christopher Wren. Traitors' heads continued to be displayed on it, as they had been on its predecessor, until the mid-1700s.

During the 19th century, Child's Bank beside Temple Bar, began to use the room above it for storage of their ledgers. By the late 1800s, Temple Bar was 'a bone in the throat of Fleet Street' and it became obvious that it had to be removed in order alleviate impossible traffic congestion. Bought by wealthy brewer, Henry Meux, it remained at his country estate in Hertfordshire until its return to the City in 2004 when it was re-erected beside St Paul's Cathedral.

Fleet Street in the thirties, with horse traffic still in evidence and the cart on the left loaded with newsprint. This is a rare view looking west – most photographers pointed their cameras in the opposite direction. The sometimes impressive newspaper buildings remain but are now occupied by other types of business following the mass exodus of the news trade in the 1980s. The last connection of the news trade with Fleet Street was broken on 15 June 2005 when Reuters news agency moved out.

GRESHAM STREET and LOTHBURY

Guildhall Yard c. 1756 showing John Croxton's early 15th century hall and its porch adorned with statues of the Discipline, Justice, Fortitude and Temperance. The chapel to the right of the hall was used as a law courts after the Reformation and demolished in the 1820s.

Gresham Street has only existed since 1845 when various smaller streets were joined together to become one. The streets did not form a straight line from east to west so corners and junctions were evened out to create the new thorough-fare. The most easterly section of what is now Gresham Street is shown on maps from the 1500s to 1800s under various names: Cateaton Street, Ketton Street, Catte Street. It ran as far west as Aldermanbury where it became Lad Lane, which stretched to Wood Street where Maiden Lane then ran to Foster Lane. The most westerly section was called St Anne's Lane.

Two important sites in the Roman city were situated just north of the present street's line. The Roman amphitheatre, covering present day Guildhall Yard, was first constructed in 70AD entirely of wood, with exterior dimensions roughly the size of a soccer pitch. Around 122AD it was enlarged to seat 6,000 people, the exterior walls and entrance areas then being built in Kentish ragstone. Although little evidence has been found of what entertainments were staged in the arena, it is thought that gladiatorial combat did take place, and bones of boars, bears and wolves have been found in excavations. The amphitheatre was probably also used for soldiers' drill and exercise as the fort stood only 65ft (20ms) away to the northwest. Constructed at roughly the same time as this second phase of the amphitheatre, the fort was possibly part of city improvements to coincide with a visit by Emperor Hadrian in 122AD. Both buildings were then a considerable distance from the main area of settlement and public buildings situated to the southeast. The 12 acres of the fort stretched across present day London Wall to the north; today's Wood Street follows the line of the central road running through it from north to south. Part of the fort wall and remains of a turret can still be seen just off Gresham Street, in Noble Street.

On the south side of Gresham Street before the building at No. 30 was recently constructed archaeological digs in 2001 had unearthed a complex Roman water wheel system, consisting of a three metre high treadmill, wheels, chains and buckets. Capable of raising thousands of litres a day from a well, it dated from late in the first century, and could have supplied water for baths, and for industries such as brewing and dyeing. During the same excavations, remains were found of a Jewish mikvah, or ritual bath. In 1128 'a street of the Jews' is first mentioned when a community was established by a scholar Rabbi Joseph. At this time, Aaron of Lincoln, said to be the richest man in England, owned a house in Lothbury. The Great Synagogue stood in Old Jewry where today's street name acts as a reminder of a community expelled from England in 1290, by edict of King Edward I.

St Lawrence Jewry church takes its name from its situation on the edge of the Jewish area. The church has existed from the late 12th century and from 1294 until the 19th century it belonged to the masters and scholars of Balliol College, Oxford who owned the land here. The present Wren church was noted particularly for its superb interior woodwork, all lost when the church was gutted in 1940. The east end exterior is particularly ornate, flanking the entrance into Guildhall Yard. The City of London has always been governed from this area. Evidence exists of a 13th century building here and, although its location is unknown, King Henry II in the early 1100s summoned the citizens to meet in 'a great hall' which also could have been on the same site. The surviving 15th century hall has required several replacement roofs over the centuries, one following 1666 and again after the Blitz. The open aspect of Guildhall today is a product of the last 30 years. Before the 1970s additions to the west side of Guildhall Yard, the buildings were approached through a much narrower space and in the early 1400s, when the present hall was built, it would have been invisible from what was then Catte Street to the south. Fear of riots and insurrections led to the hall and all the buildings in its precincts (a chapel, library, and college of priests) being closed off from the City by a defensive gatehouse to the east of St Lawrence Jewry church, leading into a narrow yard. Originally constructed in the 1200s, the gatehouse was rebuilt when master mason John Croxton constructed the present Guildhall, completing it in 1430.

To the east of Guildhall by the late 1300s, Blackwell Hall was well established as England's prime woollen cloth market and was perhaps the most important in medieval Europe. Almost all cloth in the country had to pass through it before export, acting therefore, as a major source of revenue for the City. Taking its

The warehouses of Messrs J. & R. Morley in the 1840s on the south side of Gresham Street at the corner of Milk Street. The church in the distance is St Michael Wood Street, rebuilt by Wren after the Fire and demolished in 1894.

An almost deserted Gresham Street probably on a Sunday c. 1914 with two men, one on a cycle, outside Knowles & Phillips pharmacy on the corner of Basinghall Street.

name from Sir John de Baukwell who owned the property from the 1290s, Blackwell Hall was at the peak of its importance in the 15th century when the large trading rooms within the building, named the main areas of wool production in England. It was rebuilt several times, being finally demolished in 1820.

In 1478, when the wool market was at the height of its prominence, Sir Thomas More, statesman under Henry VIII, was born in Milk Street, on the corner of where Catte Street became Lad Lane.

As well as St Lawrence Jewry, the church of St Anne and St Agnes on the corner of Noble Street survives, despite suffering war damage like the former. Before 1940, it was hidden away behind the buildings of Gresham Street and only visible through a narrow space. Today, it stands in the spacious setting of attractive gardens. On the opposite corner of Noble Street, until 1666, stood the church of St John Zachary, which was never rebuilt. The land here was owned in the mid-1100s by the canons of St Paul's Cathedral who gave it to a man called Zachary, hence the dedication. Its site is marked today by the Goldsmiths Garden, originally created by firewatchers in 1941.

Descriptions of pre-war Gresham Street conjure up a very different style of street from today. A large wool warehouse and a carpet warehouse stood on the north side to the west; several premises were connected with the rag trade; and near to St Lawrence Jewry, there were a hat seller and a model electric train shop interspersed with many solicitors' offices.

The old lanes which now make up Gresham Street were once home to three livery companies, two of which are still situated at the western end of the street. The Goldsmiths' Company have occupied a hall in what was Maiden Lane since the 1300s, as have their near neighbours the Wax Chandlers, on the same site since 16th century. A royal charter of 1327 gave the Goldsmiths the right to regulate not only gold, but also silver standards, and the responsibility for marking the metals with the King's Mark of the leopard's head. This assaying process is still carried out at their premises today.

The Goldsmiths' present hall was opened in 1835, on which occasion the Duke of Wellington and Robert Peel gave inaugural speeches. Their first home was a merchant's house, replaced by the first hall in early 1600s. Destroyed in the Great Fire and rebuilt, the Assay office was lost in a fire in 1681, when all records of early silvermakers' marks were tragically destroyed.

The Wax Chandlers' trade was in beeswax candles for the church and the wealthy, together with sealing wax for documents. Their present building post-dates World War II when their 17th century hall was lost.

The Haberdashers' Company occupied the site on the opposite side of the street from the 1470s. The company originally made coarse linen cloth that was worn under armour but later traded in pins, ribbons, buttons and laces. Their second home, a Hall built after the Great Fire in the 1670s, was lost in World War II. In the 1990s, the Haberdashers' Company moved from this site to Smithfield.

Several notable coaching inns were located in this area of the City north of St Paul's. The Windmill Inn in Old Jewry was an important hostelry in the 1500s with stabling for 120 horses. Playwright Ben Jonson set scenes here in his play 'Every Man in His Humour'. On the corner of Aldermanbury and what was Lad Lane stood The Swan with Two Necks, a terminus for northbound coaches. By the 19th century, it had become a respectable family hotel, where one could obtain bed, breakfast and dinner. Pickfords, the removals company, founded in the 1600s was running passenger coaches by this time from Manchester to the inn, six days a week. The inn's name was derived from the ancient custom of 'swan upping' which takes place on the Thames each summer when swans are marked according to their ownership. Those belonging to the Vintners' Company receive two 'nicks' to their beak; hence, the name was originally 'the Swan with Two Nicks'. Opposite, on the south side of Lad Lane and corner of Milk Street, Sweetings Restaurant, now situated in Queen Victoria Street, began life in 1830 as a fish and oyster merchant; their first restaurant opened in Milk Street six years later.

Lothbury in Victorian times with the church of St Margaret's in the centre.

At its eastern end, Gresham Street joins Lothbury which runs along the north side of the Bank of England. The origin of the name is unknown; it may be from a 'burgh' or manor belonging to a family called Lotha or a derivation of 'lod', a drain leading into a stream. The River Walbrook, used by the Romans as a prime water source, now runs under Lothbury from north to south. The stream has not been visible since the 15th century when it was covered due to its polluted waters caused by 'the divers filth and dung thrown therein by persons who have houses along the said course'.

For three hundred years, until 1853, the Founders' Hall stood in Lothbury. Before 1666, they leased part of their premises to companies of merchant adventurers including East India merchants and also to the Company of Brown Bread Makers. In 1569, they were allowed to join the Bakers' Company, primarily only for makers of white bread, then considered superior and only for the wealthy. The founders worked in brass and tinplate, making small items such as candlesticks, pots and pans. The writer Daniel Defoe, in the 1700s, even suggested that the street was so called, due to the 'loathsome' noise made by their trade.

Leading off Lothbury to the north is the narrow lane, Tokenhouse Yard. Tokens were private coins given as change by tradesmen in denominations of less than the official coinage. They were stamped with the name and trade sign and could only be used in the same shop or those in the immediate neighbourhood. In the 1630s, the Token House was set up here to take official control of the system, the practice dying out during the reign of Charles II.

HOLBORN VIADUCT and HOLBORN

The Fleet Market in the early 19th century.

The church of St Sepulchre-without-Newgate is situated on the crossroads diagonally opposite the Old Bailey at the eastern end of the street which became known as Holborn Viaduct after the vast cast-iron bridge opened over the Fleet River valley in November 1869.

The name Holborn means the 'old bourne' or stream, a tributary of the River Fleet. The church is said to have been given its dedication by 12th century crusading knights and like the church outside the walls of Jerusalem, was known as the Church of the Holy Sepulchre. The church's main bells are those mentioned in the nursery rhyme 'Oranges and Lemons' – 'when will you pay me, say the bells of Old Bailey'.

Buried in the church in 1631 was Captain John Smith, mapmaker of the New World, one of the early leaders of the settlement at Jamestown, Virginia, whose life was saved by Pocahontas, and in 1944, the ashes of Sir Henry Wood, founder of the BBC Promenade Concerts, were interred here.

Opposite the church, on the south side of the street, the imposing edifice at Nos. 1–10 Holborn Viaduct, occupied by offices and shops today, was built in 1874 as Spiers and Pond's Hotel. Designed in the French Renaissance style, it rises to an impressive seven storeys with a high ornate roof. Next door until 1941 stood the Holborn Viaduct Hotel. It had been built in 1874, when the London, Chatham & Dover Railway built Holborn Viaduct Station. It was considered the most luxurious hotel in the City, its interior resplendent with marble pillars and glittering ornamentation. During World War I, it was used by the Government and then as offices for the next twenty years.

Before the early 1800s, the line of the street west to Holborn was quite different. After passing through the Newgate, the section of the road running past St Sepulchre's church was called Hartrow Street. The main route to the west followed Snow Hill, then a longer steep and twisting street which meandered north before turning west again to cross the Fleet River and link with Holborn Hill. In 1802–3, a new section of road, Skinner Street, running directly west from Giltspur Street, was constructed to bypass this circuitous route via Snow Hill.

Holborn Bridge looking west c. 1830 before the construction of Holborn Viaduct.

On Snow Hill once stood a coaching inn of great renown, The Saracen's Head, again allegedly named by the crusaders. It was described by Dickens in Nicholas Nickleby as the place where Nicholas met the sadistic Yorkshire schoolmaster, Wackford Squeers and left with him for Yorkshire: *its portals guarded by two Saracens' heads and shoulders ... when you walk up the yard, you will see the booking office on your left and the tower of St Sepulchre's church darting abruptly into the sky on your right and a gallery of bedrooms on both sides ...* The inn supplied *solid lunches, stage-coach dinners and unusually substantial breakfasts.* Snow Hill police station stands on its site today. Prior to 1940, outside the Snow Hill offices of Ormiston and Glass, decorative terracotta panels showed scenes from the novel.

In 1688, John Bunyan died suddenly of 'a violent fever' at the house of a friend on Snow Hill and was buried at Bunhill Fields on City Road. Daniel Defoe wrote in the 1700s of a water conduit on the hill, of which by then there were several in the City. He described the water from 'distant springs' which was 'very sweet and good'. There was a railway station at Snow Hill from 1874 to 1916, a stop between Ludgate Hill and Farringdon with a link also running east to Moorgate. Turnagain Lane once ran from Snow Hill as far as the Fleet River, so called as once the riverbank had been reached, there was no alternative but to retrace one's steps. A small section survives to the east of Farringdon Street.

A little further to the west, Snow Hill became Holborn Bridge as it crossed the Fleet River, which flowed southwards to here from its source in Hampstead. The section south of Holborn Bridge had become so squalid and polluted that in 1733 it was covered over as far as where the Fleet Bridge crossed the river at today's Ludgate Circus. Six years later, the Stocks Market for meat and vegetables was moved here when its original site was cleared for the planned construction of the Mansion House. The Fleet Market was housed in one storey shops, co-incidentally also designed by George Dance the Elder, the architect of Mansion House, and were built over the covered river on what became known as Farringdon Street. They were laid out in two rows with covered walkways and a central clock tower.

Journeys from the west into the City at this point had always proved difficult, if not treacherous. The roads approaching the valley of the Fleet were steep and dangerous for heavily laden horse drawn carriages, having to brake going downhill and to struggle to climb up on the other side. Eventually construction began of the viaduct to span the valley to speed up traffic to and from the City. A broadsheet of the day commented:

Horses and donkeys will caper like fleas,
No more sore shoulders and broken knees.
The animal society may take their ease.
Goodbye to the once Holborn Hill.

The vast scale of the construction site for the Holborn Viaduct looking west towards Holborn in 1869. Hoardings advertise the 'new' St Pancras station which opened the previous year.

Completed and opened by Queen Victoria in 1869, Holborn Viaduct had taken six years to build and at a cost of over £2 million. There were originally four corner buildings to the viaduct, but today only the two to the south survive, the

other two having been destroyed in World War II bombing. Each was dedicated to an historical figure in the City's history, and bore their statues. Those to survive are of Henry Fitzailwyn, first mayor of the City in 1189, and Thomas Gresham, founder of the Royal Exchange; those lost were of Sir Hugh Myddleton, pioneer of the New River scheme to supply water to the City in the early 17th century and Sir William Walworth, Lord Mayor at the time of the Peasants' Revolt in 1381.

The building of the viaduct involved the demolition of much of the surrounding area including the notorious slums of Field Lane which ran off to the north, opposite where the City Temple (built 1874) stands today. It is here that Dickens set Fagin's den in Oliver Twist: *Near to the spot on which Snow Hill and Holborn meet, there opens ... a narrow and dismal alley ... the emporium of petty larceny, visited at early morning and setting-in of dusk by silent merchants, who traffic in dark back parlours ... stores of old iron and bones, and heaps of mildewy fragments of woollen-stuff and linen, rust and rot in the grimy cellars.*

A view looking east from Holborn Circus. Note the confined space around Prince Albert's statue compared to today, and the group of ornate gas lamps. The church of St Sepulchre without Newgate is visible in the distance, the tower of St Andrew's above the buildings on the right.

Construction of the viaduct cut across the graveyard of St Andrew's Holborn and thousands of bodies were re-buried in Ilford, Essex. In the medieval church, Henry Wriothesley, the Earl of Southampton and patron of Shakespeare, had been baptised in 1545 and although it survived the Great Fire, the church was rebuilt by Wren in the 1680s, incorporating its 15th century tower. It was the largest parish church that he designed. The old tower was refaced in Portland stone and heightened in 1703. In 1799, the engineer Marc Brunel married Sophie Kingdom here, and in 1817 Isaac Disraeli brought his twelve year old son Benjamin for baptism, with the purpose of making him eligible for the higher education which was not then available to Jews. One night in 1827, Dr William Marsden found a young girl who had collapsed, dying in the churchyard. Her death, following his thwarted efforts to admit her to a hospital, led to his founding what became the Royal Free Hospital, initially in Hatton Garden, where the poor were given free access, without letters of recommendation.

St Andrew's was severely damaged in World War II; many of the 18th century fittings today, such as the font, pulpit and part of the organ case were moved here in the 1950s from the Foundling Hospital for Abandoned Children in Bloomsbury after its buildings were demolished. The tomb of the Hospital's founder, Thomas Coram (d. 1751) was also moved and now rests at the west end of the church. To the north of the church, much of the land was owned by the Bishop of Ely from the late 1200s to the 1770s. Only the chapel of his palace, now St Etheldreda's church in Ely Place, survives.

The City limits extend westward along Holborn almost to the junction with Gray's Inn Road to what had been known since the 1100s as Holborn Bars. Today, the boundary, originally where duty was levied on traffic coming into the City, is marked by two silver dragons, one on each side of the road. Here Holborn is particularly wide part due to the existence, before 1867, of a block of buildings called Middle Row which stood in the centre of the street, just west of Holborn Bars.

Off Holborn and just inside the City, four Inns of Chancery were situated: Staple Inn, Barnard's Inn and Thavies Inn to the south and Furnival's Inn to the north. Although their origins are contemporaneous with the Inns of Court in the 1300s, they never had the same status and were initially where young aspiring lawyers began their training. Staple and Baynard's were linked with Gray's Inn; the other two with Lincoln's Inn. By the 1600s, their educational role began to decline and the Inns of Chancery became the domain of solicitors and attorneys who were by then being excluded from the Inns of Court. Gradually their role diminished until they were closed during the early 19th century. Their property was then leased out and Charles Dickens rented rooms in Furnival's Inn between 1834–7. It was whilst living here that he wrote most of Pickwick Papers and married his wife, Catherine. On its site in the late 18th century, the magnificent red-brick and terracotta headquarters of Prudential Assurance, designed by Alfred Waterhouse, architect of the Natural History Museum, were built. Begun in 1879, it was not completed until 1906. Thavies Inn was the most easterly. Before the creation of St Andrew Street (1860s) leading to Shoe Lane, its garden was joined to the churchyard of St Andrew's. Only a street name today recalls its site.

The 15th century hall of Baynard's Inn still exists to the south whilst the dramatic black and white timbered façade of Staple Inn, dating from 1586, faces Holborn near Gray's Inn Road. It was reconstructed in 1887 and to enable its survival had a steel frame inserted in 1937. The name 'Staple Inn' may be derived from a medieval market or 'staple' where wool was traded or from the old English 'stapel' – a post – perhaps referring to an earlier timber aisled hall.

At the eastern end of Holborn next to the Prudential Building stood Gamage's department store, opened in 1878 by Arthur Walter Gamage in a tiny building only five feet wide. His motto 'Tall Oaks From Little Acorns Grow' was written above the door and proved to be prophetic as the store's success led to the acquisition of several surrounding buildings, which meant shopping here involved the negotiation of various stairs, narrow doorways, ramps and passageways leading from one building to its neighbour. Gamage's sold practically everything. It included a zoological and a motoring department and was well known for vast mail order catalogues including, in 1913, one of the first Christmas catalogues produced, with 500 pages of toys and gifts. The store closed in March 1972.

Holborn Circus looking west in 1910
The awnings outside Gamages store can be seen on the right of the street. Wallis & Co on the left advertises linens and blankets and has a display of parasols hanging outside the shop. A man in an invalid carriage risks the traffic to the left of the statue whilst a sign on the lamp post urges drivers to exercise 'Caution' and 'Drive Slowly'.

LEADENHALL STREET

The grand East India Company building dominated this part of Leadenhall Street and is seen here in 1837. This was their second building from the 1790s. The Ionic portico was adorned with sculpture, a large statue of Britannia surmounting the pediment.

Opposite An engraving from 1814 of houses on the south side of Leadenhall Street. An inn or business trading at the sign of The Cock occupies an unusual building on the right where corbels supporting the upper storey are carved as human figures. By the door, a man in Chinese dress appears to be entertaining a group of children or selling his goods while a workman repairs the road.

In the early 1400s, the grand house of the Neville family stood at the western end of Leadenhall Street. It was a hall with a roof covered in lead, unusual for a domestic dwelling of the period and this 'leaden hall' gave the street its name. The market also developed at this time, particularly for poultry and dairy produce, and where those from outside London, called 'foreigners', could sell their wares. A map of 1676 shows the market area as being divided into four separate sections though Daniel Defoe in 1725 describes its three squares or courtyards. The main market was the Beef Market, with gates into Leadenhall Street and Gracechurch Street; on Wednesdays, this market sold hides, skins, leather and shoemakers' tools. The second area, the Fish Market was also a place where 'country higlers' sold butter, eggs and country fare – a 'higler' being a 17th century name for an itinerant dealer. 'Town butchers' also sold mutton and veal in this part of the market. The third section, the Butter Market, contained 'all sorts of 'higglary goods', and sections for poultry, bacon and herbs. During the 18th century, a goose named 'Old Tom' became legendary at Leadenhall; having escaped the slaughter of thousands of geese, he continued to live here, fed by local inns, and on his death and after a 'lying in state', was buried in the market.

Opposite Leadenhall Market 1930 showing City businessmen together with women shopping in a working market with open stalls, carts, delivery vehicles, milk churns and baskets.

The splendid Victorian buildings that exist today date from 1881 when Sir Horace Jones designed them for the City Corporation which continues to administer the market after 600 years. These buildings today lie over the eastern section of one of the most important areas of the Roman city – the forum and basilica developed in the 1st century AD. The forum was the City's business centre containing shops and offices where traders and merchants met. Forming the northern edge of the Forum, the Basilica at 400ft (150m) long was the most impressive such structure north of the Alps. It acted as the town hall where the local senate met and housed the courts of justice.

Throughout the 18th and 19th centuries, the street was dominated by the imposing monumental building which housed the East India Company. A classical style edifice with a grand Ionic portico, it extended practically along the entire length of Lime Street from the corner of Leadenhall Street, occupying the present site of Lloyds of London. The company, founded in 1600, first leased a house belonging to Lord Craven here in 1650. It had been formed initially to challenge the Dutch-Portuguese monopoly of the spice trade from the East Indies. Eventually establishing bases in India, it extended its power by force, becoming a vast administrative and military concern until the British government took charge of all Indian affairs in 1858. Charles Lamb, the 19th century writer working here as a clerk wrote, 'My printed works were my recreations – my true works may be found on the shelves in Leadenhall Street, filling some hundred folios'. The company's headquarters building here in the City housed a concert hall, Indian paintings, a library of Indian literature and a museum, which during the 19th century, was open to the public on Saturdays from 11 till 3. Most of the collection was transferred to the Victoria and Albert Museum when the company was wound up. It includes Tippoo's Tiger, an automaton of painted wood, in the shape of a tiger pinning a British soldier to the ground. It is coincidental that during some 19th century building work, a superb piece of Roman mosaic floor was unearthed, showing Bacchus riding on a tiger. Normally depicted seated on a leopard, the tiger refers to the myth that Bacchus visited India. This is now housed in the British Museum as are the magnificent Buddhist sculptures from Amaravati in India which were also once in the East India Company's collection.

A little further to the east at the corner of Billiter Street the office of the Royal Africa Company stood throughout the late 17th and early 18th centuries. It had been set up by the government in 1672, controlling company forts on the West African coast in order to protect the interests of slave traders. Ships could take on food and water at the forts, and select slaves from those held in company dungeons, rather than have to find them elsewhere. Merchants of the City of London initially held a monopoly over the trade for the first 25 years, but this was repealed due to opposition from other cities such as Bristol. The Royal Africa Company ceased to exist in 1750.

This south eastern corner of the City has traditionally been the place where shipping and insurance companies were concentrated. P & O (Peninsular & Oriental Steam Navigation Company) had offices here and the Cunard White Star building, built for the shipping line in the 1930s at 88 Leadenhall Street, was not demolished until the late 1990s.

Leadenhall Street from the eastern end in 1911. Two doors along from Carton's the tailor, M. Etheridge advertises 'Artificial Teeth' and next door is a sign enquiring 'Anything the Matter?' The premises are listed as being occupied by Bousfield Stanley, physician and surgeon. Buildings on the left of the street are occupied by importers of Turkish tobacco.

In 1925, Lloyds (see EASTCHEAP and CORNHILL) moved into a building on the old site of the East India Company building. Designed by Sir Edwin Cooper, the main entrance arch of this building survives, facing Leadenhall Street and incorporated into Lloyd's present building.

In 1903, the Baltic Exchange (see THREADNEEDLE STREET) moved into their magnificent new building in St Mary Axe. Typical of grand City architecture of this era, it boasted marble halls, a glass domed roof and an exterior pediment depicting Britannia and Neptune. It was demolished after damage by a terrorist bomb in 1992.

St Mary Axe takes its name from a curious legend associated with it and a church that stood here until 1561. The story tells of a king of England who allowed his daughter Ursula to travel abroad, provided that she was accompanied by her 11,000 handmaidens. They journeyed as far as the Rhineland where they encountered Attila the Hun who slaughtered them all using three axes. The church, founded in the late 1100s was said to possess one of the axes and was referred to by John Stow as St Mary the Virgin and St Ursula and the Eleven Thousand Virgins. Author of a 'Survey of London' Stow is buried in St Andrew Undershaft situated at the corner of St Mary Axe and Leadenhall Street, and one of the few City churches to escape the Great Fire. A monument inside shows him as if seated at a desk, holding a real quill pen which is replaced by the Lord Mayor in a special ceremony every few years. Penniless in old age, he asked King James I for permission to beg, but was only allowed to do so outside the City limits where no-one knew him. He died in 1605.

Beside the church, an extremely high maypole shaft was erected every year, hence its dedication. For the rest of the year, it was stored under the eaves of a house in Shaft Stairs, off the north side of Leadenhall Street, until in 1547 it was chopped up and burnt after being declared heathen by the priest of nearby St Katherine Cree. In this church, further along the street to the east, the 'Lion Sermon' is preached annually, usually in October. It is done in memory of John Gayer, a wealthy merchant who in 1610, while travelling in Middle East, lost his caravan and knelt to pray. Looking up, he saw a lion advancing. Terrified, he asked for salvation, and when the lion turned and left, he vowed he would give money to his church and have a sermon preached every year in thanks.

Beside St Katherine Cree (its name Creechurch is probably a corruption of Christchurch), runs Creechurch Lane. Here in 1657, a synagogue was established in a private house after a small community of Sephardi Jews was officially allowed to resettle in the City by Oliver Cromwell, for the first time since 1290, when Jews had been expelled from London under an edict of King Edward I. They moved to the newly built Bevis Marks synagogue when they outgrew the house in 1701. The church itself was founded in the 13th century by the Augustinian monks of Holy Trinity Priory situated at the eastern end of Leadenhall Street, who decide they no longer wanted their services disturbed by local parishioners. The first London priory to be closed in Henry VIII's destruction of religious houses in 1530s, Holy Trinity was pulled down and its stones sold – all that is, apart from a section of a pointed arch from the south wall which survived and is still visible inside number 76.

On the opposite corner stands the Aldgate Pump dating from 1870 with its spout in the shape of a brass dog's head. Water from a local well provided water for a pump on this site from the 13th century for 600 years until a report of 1876 into the unhygienic quality of the water and its link to disease finally led to the well's closure. In 1876 the pump was then connected to much cleaner mains water supplied from the New River Company works to the north of the City in Islington and Stoke Newington.

Leadenhall Market, south side, in 2005.

LONDON WALL and MOORGATE

The imposing structure of Bedlam Hospital seen from the north. The gardens occupied the site of today's Finsbury Circus. The hospital moved to Lambeth in 1815 when these buildings were demolished.

London Wall is really a street of two halves. The eastern part from Coleman Street to Old Broad Street was originally a medieval thoroughfare, though not known as London Wall until the 1540s. By the 18th century, the street is shown on maps extending as far west as Wood Street, but it then followed a route slightly more to the north west, along the line of present day St Alphage Gardens and following more closely the line of the Roman wall, as the eastern part of the street had always done. This section of London Wall, west of Moorgate was much narrower than its eastern end during the first part of the 20th century and in fact, Fore Street was the more major traffic route. During World War II bombing, this area was the part of the City that suffered most devastation. Plans were drawn up in 1955 for a new urban scheme for a dual carriageway, lined with office blocks linked by overhead walkways, with pedestrians moving above the traffic. Known originally as Route XI, a new and dramatically altered London Wall was built in the 1960s.

After about 150 years of Roman occupation the decision was made to encircle the city with a wall. It was complete by about 210AD. Two miles long, probably about 19ft (6m) high and roughly 9ft (2.7m) thick, it must have been a forbidding barrier to citizens and outsiders alike. The western end of present day London Wall runs east-west through the site of the Roman fort, Wood Street dissecting it from north to south. (see GRESHAM STREET). The Cripplegate that stood at the present junction of Wood Street and St Alphage Garden was the north gate from the fort but unlike other gates, did not lead to an important road out of the City. It may have been named after a medieval underground passageway, a 'crepel 'or 'cripule', which was part of the gate, or simply after the cripples who begged in the vicinity. The city gate at Moorgate to the east was not of Roman origin but created in the early 1400s.

CRIPPLE-GATE.

Just outside Cripplegate, in 1177 the only Jewish cemetery in England was recorded. In 1558, ten days after her accession to the throne, Queen Elizabeth I, in an open carriage and wearing a dress of deep purple, entered the City for the first time as Queen. The area beyond Cripplegate and outside the wall was known as an area of criminals, outcasts, prostitutes, unscrupulous merchants and dubious tradesmen in the Middle Ages. The area was spared destruction in 1666, as was its church, St Giles Cripplegate, burial place of John Milton (d. 1674) and Martin Frobisher, sailor and explorer (d. 1594). Three centuries later however, the Great Cripplegate Fire of 1897, starting in an ostrich feather warehouse, destroyed 127 surrounding buildings. In nearby Fore Street, the first bomb of World War II fell in the City on 25th August 1940. Within a year, the area with its narrow Victorian streets, home to milliners, stationers, hosiery and dress shops and textile merchants, furriers and hatters had been swept away. A wasteland developed; wild flowers and vegetation grew and the Home Guard trained in the ruins. During the 1950s, plans began to evolve to recreate the Barbican as we know it today.

Until their destruction in this period, two streets existed of which now there is no trace. Silver Street ran between Noble Street and Wood Street, just to the south of present day London Wall. Its name first appeared in the 1500s as being a street of fine houses where silversmiths lived. At No. 24 from the 1670s, stood the Hall of the Parish Clerks Company who had existed since the 1200s. Administering relief to the parish poor, they also performed religious Mystery plays prior to the Reformation, and as accomplished musicians, often provided music for entertainments and funerals. Roughly halfway along its length, Silver Street joined Monkwell Street which then ran north, crossing today's London Wall as far as where Monkwell Square, created after World War II, is situated. A church stood at this junction with Silver Street until the Great Fire. It was first referred to as St Olave de Mukewellstrate in 1181 but later as St Olave Silver Street, becoming the parish church of the silversmiths' trade and reputedly containing a figure of Christ wearing silver shoes. In a house at this corner, William Shakespeare is reported to have lodged in 1602. The premises were over a shop belonging to the Mountjoy family, French Huguenot makers of wigs and jewelled head dresses. Conveniently nearby in Golden Lane stood the Fortune Theatre, built 1600 by Edward Alleyn and Philip Henslowe and in existence for just over 60 years.

Monkwell Street had been home to the Barber Surgeons' Company since the 1400s. Barbers had since early times assisted monks in surgery and had remained superior in rank to surgeons, after monks were forbidden involvement in the shedding of blood in a 12th century Papal edict. Barbers and surgeons joined ranks with the establishment of the company in 1540. The 1630s' hall, designed by Inigo Jones, incorporated an anatomy theatre for the dissection of corpses. The ornately beautiful building in which these grisly events took place was lost in 1940.

Three other livery companies have been based in and around London Wall for as long as the Barber Surgeons: the Brewers in Addle Street since 1418, the Armourers and Brasiers on the corner of Coleman Street since 1346 and further to the east, the Carpenters' Company first leased the land on which their hall stands in 1430. Before the Great Fire at a time when most buildings were constructed from wood, the Carpenters were the master builders of the City. Although their hall managed to escape the Fire, being surrounded by extensive gardens which acted as a firebreak, the importance of their trade then diminished as a result of the new regulations which followed, requiring the use of stone and brick as building materials. In the 1870s, Throgmorton Avenue to the west of Carpenters' Hall was created as a private road running south to Drapers' Hall through the gardens which then belonged to the two companies. It still remains as a private gated road, owned by the Drapers and Carpenters. The Carpenters' Hall was rebuilt built shortly afterwards in 1880 but reduced to a shell in May 1941, when a bomb fell in London Wall, igniting a gas main. A new hall was then constructed within the surviving walls. The Brewers' Hall was totally destroyed in 1940 though the Armourers and Brasiers still occupy a building that was built in the 1840s.

The church of All Hallows London Wall, first constructed on the wall itself in the 1100s, was home to a reclusive hermit, Simon the Anchor, in the 1400s. He lived in an anchorite cell within the church. All Hallows was reconstructed to the designs of George Dance the Younger in 1765, who referred to it as 'my first child'.

The newly rebuilt church of All Hallows in the late 18th century.

A corner bastion, probably late 1300s, on what was originally the Roman City wall and at the northwest corner of the fort. To the right is Barber Surgeons' Hall (rebuilt 1969).

Further to the west, near to where Monkwell Street ran, was the church of St James in the Wall, also a hermitage and first recorded in 1189. In the late 16th century, it became the Lambe Chapel, established by William Lambe of the Clothworkers' Company. Part of its crypt still survives under the tower of All Hallows Staining in Mark Lane, to where it was moved in the 1870s.

Immediately to the north of the 1960 dual carriageway section of London Wall, some of the 14th century ruins of the tower and north transept of Elsing Spital are visible. Founded by William Elsing as a hospital for a hundred blind men, the site had been formerly occupied by the Priory of St Mary within Cripplegate; the name 'spital' is an abbreviation of 'hospital'.

After the hospital's closure in 1536, its chapel was taken over by the parishioners of the nearby church of St Alphage. There were therefore, three churches actually constructed on or up against the wall itself. The church no longer exists but in the street that bears its name, St Alphage Gardens, a section of the city wall still remains. In 1623, on the site of where part of Elsing Spital had stood, the religious institution of Sion College was founded. It acted as a society for Anglican priests of the City of London, in brick buildings surrounding a courtyard, and including almshouses for 'twenty poor persons'. By 1650, its vast library contained 6,000 volumes. Used largely as a resource for the clergy, it was also a copyright library from 1710 to 1836. It had grown to 40,000 books and manuscripts by 1850, when it was available for use by 'respectable persons of all classes'. The College moved from the City to the Victoria Embankment in the 1880s. Today, its collection still survives as part of King's College Library.

The Bethlehem Royal Hospital or 'Bedlam' occupied by far the largest building in London Wall between 1676 and 1815 stretching 540ft (165m) from present-day Moorgate, eastward to Blomfield Street. Having moved from Bishopsgate, the Hospital occupied a majestic building designed by city surveyor Robert Hooke, and was compared by diarist John Evelyn to the Palace of the Tuileries in Paris. It is said that Louis XIV was so insulted that he got his revenge by building an asylum in Paris based on St James's Palace in London. Its gardens covered the area of today's Finsbury Circus. Over the entrances, Caius Cibber carved two enormous male figures representing Melancholy and Madness. Described by Alexander Pope as 'Cibber's brazen brainless brothers', they are today in the Museum of London. Wealthy sightseers were admitted to observe the chained patients, on payment of an entry fee. Until 1766 when the practice was abolished, it had become one the 'must-sees' for visitors to London.

First constructed in the 1400s, the gate at Moorgate was rebuilt in 1672 as an imposing three-storey structure, though the area beyond it still remained rural

in character. The area of Moorfields and Finsbury described by William Fitzstephen in 1174 as the place where citizens sped on their animal shinbone skates across the frozen marsh 'as swift as a bird in flight' is still shown on a map of 1559 as fields with grazing cattle. It was also one of the places outside the City walls called tenter grounds where those involved in cloth production could spread their newly dyed fabric out to dry, stretching it and pulling it taut, pegging it down with hooks, and so originating the expression 'to be on tenterhooks' or to be subject to tension and stress.

In 1598, John Stow wrote that Moorfields was 'a garden to the city ... for citizens to walk and take the air and for merchants' maids to dry clothes in'.

A rough road or causeway led out of the gate into the fields, having been constructed soon after 1400, when refuse was dumped to help with drainage and to raise the ground. On 18th century maps, this part of the road north of London Wall was known as Finsbury. Just outside the gate stood the Swan and Hoop tavern and stables, and here in 1795 the poet John Keats was born, his father being the chief ostler at the stable. When in 1840, the road was extended south towards the Bank, it became known as Moorgate Street and simply Moorgate by the middle of the 20th century. Built to the east of Coleman Street, it cut through old alleys running west to east – Great Swan Alley, Whites Alley, Great Bell Alley and Kings Arms Yard, and was part of a scheme of roads eventually leading to the new London Bridge.

The eastern part of London Wall in 1933 looking east with All Hallows church in the distance. This end of London Wall did not suffer the degree of World War Two bombing suffered by the stretch between Moorgate and Aldersgate Street and some of the buildings survive, particularly on the north side.

An engraving by Thomas Shotterboys of 1842 with St Martin within Ludgate on the left. The view is from the corner of St Martin's Court, now called Ludgate Court. Two pupils of Christ's Hospital School, then situated in Newgate Street to the north of St Paul's, are shown on the right of the street.

LUDGATE HILL

The high ground at the eastern end of the street, which the cathedral of St Paul has occupied for 1400 years, was an early important vantage point for the Roman founders of the city. The area has proved rich in Roman finds. In the 17th century, a tombstone dedicated to Vivius Marcianus and showing a life-size Roman soldier was unearthed near St Martin's Church, and in the early 1800s, a column was found, built in honour of the eighteen year old wife of a slave, Anencletus. Both can be seen in the Museum of London.

68

At Ludgate Hill's western end, and running at right angles to it along the line of New Bridge Street and Farringdon Street today, flowed the River Fleet, forming a natural defensive western boundary to the Roman city. Its name is taken from a Saxon word for a 'creek' or 'tidal inlet'. Rising in Hampstead, it also provided a source of fresh water for the early citizens, an alternative to the brackish waters of the Thames. The city gate stood across the hill just east of the road known as Old Bailey. It is said to be named in memory of a legendary King Lud supposedly living around 66BC, although the name could be a corruption of Floodgate or Fleetgate. Statues of King Lud, his sons and of Queen Elizabeth I adorned a new gateway completed in 1586. It was demolished, along with most of the City gates in 1760. At this time, the statues were taken to the church of St Dunstan in the West in Fleet Street, where they can still be seen on the exterior of the church.

On a site that would have been just inside the wall and the gate stands St Martin within Ludgate. The earlier church of St Martin, destroyed in the Great Fire, was first recorded in the 12th century whilst on the summit of the hill, another church which no longer exists suffered the same fate – St Gregory by St Paul's. Originally built in 1010, it stood at the south western corner of the old Gothic St Paul's Cathedral, roughly where the statue of Queen Anne stands outside Wren's cathedral today. When the cathedral was damaged due to its immense spire being struck by lightning in 1561, services were held in St Gregory's. Local parishioners thought highly of their church and were enraged when Inigo Jones wanted to demolish it to make way for his rebuilding of the cathedral porch in the 1640s. Finally the Great Fire saw the end of St Gregory's. It was never rebuilt, probably due to Wren's grand plans for his new St Paul's, and after the rebuilding of the City the area became a very fashionable shopping place.

Even until 1940, businesses and shops situated in large Victorian buildings faced the front of the cathedral but were eventually lost in bombing raids. The large textile warehouse of Hitchcock and Williams stood near to Evans' Restaurant, well used by cathedral clergy. In the early 1900s, at the corner of Ludgate Hill, stood Goodman's Dentists, advertising in large white letters on the windows of their three-storey facade 'Teeth, complete set one guinea; single tooth 2/6; five years guarantee; painless gas extractions 5/-'

Hidden away off Ludgate Hill to the north the Worshipful Company of Stationers have occupied their hall since 1673. The company was formed in 1403 when those involved in publishing and production of manuscripts and books set up fixed stalls in the churchyard of St Paul's and thus traded from 'stationary' positions in contrast to the many itinerant vendors of the day. Their hall was destroyed in the Great Fire when thousands of valuable books that were stored both within and also in the Cathedral for safekeeping, fuelled the inferno. Compulsory registration of all published works at Stationers' Hall ended in 1695, though registration here still ensured copyright protection until 1911, when this became automatic.

On the east bank of the River Fleet and to the north of Ludgate Hill stood the notorious Fleet Prison. It existed from 1100s until 1840s, and was primarily for debtors. It was famous from the early 1600s for quick 'Fleet Marriages'

performed without a licence, initially in the prison's chapel but eventually also in nearby inns. Some 6,500 such unions were taking place every year in the 1740s, mainly involving labourers and artisans from surrounding poor parishes, soldiers and sailors. The marriages proved popular as they were cheap, quick, had no need for parental consent and were often entered into as a result of a bride's pregnancy. They were finally made illegal in 1753.

A bridge had existed over the Fleet River since the 1400s. It was near to this crossing at the bottom of the hill where London's first daily newspaper, the Daily Courant, was published in 1702, actually on Ludgate Hill rather than Fleet Street, the newspaper world's traditional home. The paper's address at the time was given as 'against the Ditch at Fleet Bridge'.

The waters of the river had become increasingly polluted over the centuries as residents, Smithfield butchers and other tradesmen deposited their refuse into its waters and along its banks. Alexander Pope in the early 1700s wrote, 'with disemboguing streams rolls the large tribute of dead dogs to Thames.' In 1733 the section of the river north of the Fleet Bridge was covered over, with its remaining southern part from Ludgate Hill to the Thames taken underground in the 1760s. Although unseen today, the Fleet still exists in a sewer beneath the streets.

Once the river was covered, a bridge was no longer needed though congestion on Ludgate Hill remained a problem. Even as early as 1634, residents complained of a great congestion of coaches bringing audiences to the nearby Blackfriars Playhouse as 'standing together like mutton pies in a cook's oven'. All of the south side of what was then called Ludgate Street was demolished between 1860–90 in order to widen the street and it was renamed Ludgate Hill. One of

the new buildings then designed was Colcutt's terracotta and red brick City Bank of 1890, still standing on the corner of Pilgrim Court. In the same period the curved facades forming Ludgate Circus were constructed. Previously two high stone obelisks stood in the road at the junction. The first was erected in 1775 to honour the mayoralty of John Wilkes; the second, now situated in Salisbury Court off Fleet Street, was in memory of Robert Wraithman, Lord Mayor in the 1830s. Also in 1860 the London Coffee House which had stood on the east corner of Old Bailey from 1731 was demolished. James Boswell, friend and biographer of Dr Johnson, was a regular as were American visitors to London. Juries from Old Bailey were often locked into the London to enable them to reach their verdicts and in Dickens' Little Dorritt, Arthur Clemman stayed here on his arrival in London.

In 1865, the railway bridge carrying the London Chatham & Dover railway was built across Ludgate Hill, called at the time 'a miracle of clumsy and stubborn ugliness'. Two years earlier, 1000 people had signed a petition against it and *Punch* magazine had urged people to visit the site before it was destroyed for ever: *Now then, make haste, make haste, and pay a visit to Ludgate Hill and behold, for nearly the last time you will have the opportunity, the vast and celebrated Cathedral of St Paul ... In a very short time this remarkable edifice will become invisible owing to the great improvement which the march of intellect and the progress of commerce providentially force upon this Great Metropolis.*

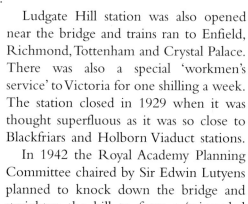

A view up the hill to St Paul's c.1908. The array of clocks on the left are outside Benson's Watchmakers and the large letters on the building a little further up the hill advertise Alexander the Great – Tailor.

Ludgate Hill station was also opened near the bridge and trains ran to Enfield, Richmond, Tottenham and Crystal Palace. There was also a special 'workmen's service' to Victoria for one shilling a week. The station closed in 1929 when it was thought superfluous as it was so close to Blackfriars and Holborn Viaduct stations.

In 1942 the Royal Academy Planning Committee chaired by Sir Edwin Lutyens planned to knock down the bridge and straighten the hill to form a 'triumphal way' but it was not finally removed until 1990.

Before the Blitz, a small cul-de-sac called Belle Sauvage Yard led northwards off Ludgate Hill to the west of Old Bailey. The name recalled the coaching inn, tavern and later hotel that stood here from the 1400s to 1873. It is referred to during its history by various names – Savage's Inn, the Bell and Hoop. Pocohontas is said to have lodged here in 1616, and later that century a rhinoceros 'lately brought from the West Indies' was put on show. Horace Walpole describes how Grinling Gibbons carved a pot of flowers over a doorway, 'so delicate in leaf and stem' that it shook with the motion of passing carriages. Hoping for increased business from the Great Exhibition, it was remodelled in 1851 and renamed the International Hotel. Demolished 20 years later, a printing works replaced it. By the 1930s, the publisher Cassells occupied the site, their building being destroyed in the Blitz.

Ludgate Hill, London,

A later view from further west showing the railway bridge that for 125 years blocked the view of St Paul's from Fleet Street. The mix of open top and closed top buses dates the picture to the mid-1920s.

NEWGATE STREET

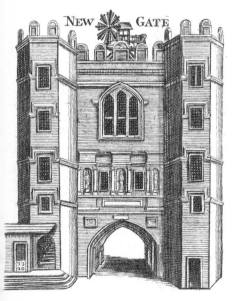

The eastern end of Newgate Street was dominated throughout the Middle Ages by the vast Franciscan monastery of the Greyfriars, followers of St Francis of Assisi. The complex ran from today's King Edward Street, westward almost as far as Giltspur Street and consisted of an impressive church over 300ft (100m) long, the Great Cloister, Little Cloister, library, hall, infirmary and gardens. Wren's church of Christchurch Greyfriars, now a ruin following World War II, serves today as a reminder of the site of the chancel of the original monastic church.

Once it was considered desirable for religious reasons to be laid to rest within the Greyfriars' precincts. Consequently, three Queens of England were buried here: Eleanor of Provence (d. 1291), wife of King Henry III; Margaret (d. 1317), second wife of King Edward I; and Isabella (d. 1358), who had been implicated in the plot to overthrow her husband, King Edward II, and in his subsequent murder in 1327.

The City Wall ran immediately to the monastery's north, and the western edge of the Greyfriars' land was also defined by the wall, as it turned south, and ran east of Giltspur Street to where the Newgate itself stood (the site of Old Bailey).

After the dissolution of Greyfriars' Monastery, the old buildings were used for various purposes, including the use of the church nave for the presses of the King's Printer. In 1553, King Edward VI founded Christ's Hospital School here for 'poor fatherless children'. The boys were educated, fed and clothed; the name 'hospital', originally used by religious foundations, shares its origin with 'hospitality' and meant to be generally cared for. Pupils wore, as they still do today, long dark blue woollen coats and yellow stockings, originally dyed with saffron, said to ward off rats. Wren's Christchurch contained steeply-raked galleries in order to accommodate all the pupils for daily services. The poet, Samuel Taylor Coleridge and the essayist Charles Lamb attended the school and were friends in the 1780s. In 1897, Christ's Hospital moved to Horsham in Sussex. Some monastic buildings still survived at this time but were demolished when the Post Office building in King Edward Street was built in 1911. The street itself had been renamed in honour of King Edward VI in 1843. Present day King Edward Street was known in earlier times by the appealing name of Stinking Lane. Here stood the hall of the Poulterers' Company in the 1600s and on Newgate Street to the south was the Shambles meat market. To the east of Stinking Lane stood the church of St Nicholas Shambles, first recorded in 1196 but demolished in the mid-1500s. At the same time, another small church, St Ewin, on the corner of nearby Warwick Lane, met the same fate. The Earls of Warwick had a substantial town house here in the 1400s.

Opposite Newgate Meat Market in 1836 which stood on the site of today's Paternoster Square and traded from the 1660s until the 1860s when the new Central Meat Market opened at nearby Smithfield. Men cleaning the market are shown on the left.

The site of the present St Paul's Underground station at the eastern end of Newgate Street in 1899 with shops selling shirts, cycles and bakery items.

Although after the Great Fire the meat market at the Shambles moved into Newgate Market, this eastern section of Newgate Street is still rather graphically named Blowbladder Street on an 18th century map of the area. Newgate Market was situated in a large square located in the area of Paternoster Square today. Hundreds of sheep were slaughtered here daily, mostly in sheds behind the butchers' stalls. The meat porters were mainly elderly women who staggered under the weight of a side of beef or a mutton carcass. Hatton writes in 1708 that the market sold meat, poultry, fruit and roots. Existing until the opening of the new Central Meat Market buildings at Smithfield in 1869, the buildings of Newgate Market were then demolished.

In the early 1700s, a small thoroughfare, Bath Street, ran north off Blowbladder Street to the east of Stinking Lane. It led to The Bagnio, described by Hatton as 'a very spacious and commodious place for sweating, hot-bathing and cupping'. Opened in 1679, it 'hath eighteen degrees of heat' and is the 'only true Bagnio after the Turkish model'. The charge was four shillings a person, 'and to show the healthfulness of sweating thus, one servant (worker) has been here now twenty-eight years, constantly attending in the heat'. Most London bagnios, however, were known for other 'services' provided for their clientele.

The Roman gate at Newgate had a double road running through it and two square towers. It gave its name to the infamous prison which existed from the 12th century and was originally joined to the gate. During the 18th century, it gained particular notoriety and was described by Henry Fielding as a 'prototype of hell'. Prisoners were confined under terrible conditions with little water and ventilation. Diseases such as 'gaol fever', a form of typhoid, were rife. Corrupt gaolers could be bribed to supply extra food, candles, or alcohol. During this period, Jack Shepherd became perhaps the prison's most notorious inmate. He managed to make several daring escapes, and had become a London celebrity by

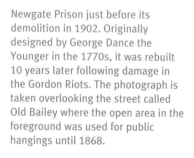

Newgate Prison just before its demolition in 1902. Originally designed by George Dance the Younger in the 1770s, it was rebuilt 10 years later following damage in the Gordon Riots. The photograph is taken overlooking the street called Old Bailey where the open area in the foreground was used for public hangings until 1868.

the time he was finally hanged. When this prison was demolished in the 1770s, parts were sold off as souvenirs, including the grating of Jack Shepherd's cell, for seven shillings and ten pence. The architect George Dance the Younger then designed a new building which was destroyed soon after its completion when anti-Catholic Gordon Rioters attacked it in 1778, allowing over 300 prisoners to escape. At this time, a small debtors' prison was built on the opposite corner to Newgate prison. Known as the Giltspur Street Comptor, its role was as a temporary prison often holding prisoners overnight by order of the city authorities. In 1869, the Viaduct Tavern was opened on the site and some of the Comptors' cells still survive in the pub's cellars. Following the Gordon Riots, the design of a replacement for Newgate in 1780 opened up a large space adjoining the buildings and so public executions, which had previously taken place at Tyburn near Marble Arch, were moved to this site. Until 1868, thousands gathered to watch the spectacle. Those with sufficient resources could obtain breakfast and a good vantage point in the Magpie and Stump pub opposite.

William Makepeace Thackeray wrote of his experiences in an essay of 1840 entitled 'Going to See A Man Hanged'. Some 40,000 people had gathered outside Newgate to see the hangman Jack Ketch execute Francois Courvoisier, a servant who had killed his master. Thackeray writes 'I fully confess that I came away down Snow Hill that morning with a disgust for murder, but it was for the murder that I saw done'. For the final five years, it was possible to travel by Underground train for the event, arriving at nearby Farringdon Street station of the Metropolitan Railway.

Following the prison's final demolition in 1902, the present Old Bailey was constructed. There had been a court house of this name next to Newgate since the 1530s, taking its name from an old tower or bailey built on the city wall in the early 1100s and known in the late 1200s, as La Baillie.

Above A view from Newgate Street towards the north transept of St Pauls Cathedral through narrow Victorian alleys lost in World War Two. A similar view has been recreated in the recent Paternoster Square development.

Left The Central Criminal Court, or Old Bailey, which replaced Newgate Prison in the early 20th century.

QUEEN VICTORIA STREET

Constructed between 1867 and 1871 to link the new Victoria Embankment to the heart of the City at Bank, Queen Victoria Street was designed to relieve traffic congestion. It had to be opened in sections, due to delays caused by the simultaneous building of the District Railway under the street.

The buildings built along the length of the new street were called 'questionable in taste' at the time. They reflected the Victorian ideals of reviving and adapting styles of the past – Gothic, Venetian and Italianate. Most were grand in scale and, at four or five storeys high, made the original thoroughfare somewhat dark and oppressive. Few survive due either to World War II bombing or more recent developments such as No. 1 Poultry, built on the site of one of the best known, John Belcher's Mansion House Buildings (1870) and known as the Mappin and Webb building after its principal occupant. This Gothic style building on its triangular site was home to many and varied trades; among the tenants in 1881 were an accountant, engineer, East India merchant, auctioneer, shirt maker, hatter, seed crusher, boot maker, bicycle manufacturer, shipping agent, tailor and the South India Gold Mining Company.

78

Two fine examples of these early buildings do however survive on the south side of the street. Next to the Mansion House, the block now housing the City Magistrates' Court was built in 1873 as the National Safe Deposit Company, the first of its kind in England. There were four storeys of vaults below the ground where the company advertised that it would keep securities, plate, jewels and deeds in 'armour clad vaults, forty feet below the building' which 'form an impregnable steel clad fortress'. A little further west, on the corner of Cannon Street, Albert Buildings remains from the 1870s. The Building News at the time described its style as 'pretentious medieval'. Part of the building still houses an original occupant, Sweetings, the fish and seafood restaurant, where inside, hat pegs act as a reminder of a time when bowler hats and even top hats were common in the City.

Beside the Mansion House runs the street named after the River Walbrook. Rising north of Moorgate, this was an important source of water for the Roman city and flowed through the centre of the earliest settlement of Londinium. On its western bank stood the Temple of Mithras though after the discovery of the Temple's remains in 1954, they were moved to their present site further along the street to the west. The religion was Christianity's strongest rival in the Roman world. Only men were involved in its rituals. Honesty, courage and purity were watchwords, and 'Dictum Meum Pactum' – my word is my bond – its motto. Worshippers descended a few steps into the rectangular aisled temple, symbolising the cave in which the Persian deity, Mithras, had sacrificed a bull.

One of the City's most ancient streets, Bucklersbury, runs north off Walbrook and was cut in two by the building of Queen Victoria Street. The manor or 'bury' of the wealthy Buckerel family, who in the 1200s supplied the City with one Lord Mayor and three Sheriffs, occupied the area. Sir Thomas More lived for a large part of his life here, moving soon after his marriage in 1505 into a house called 'The Old Barge'. The name came from its proximity to the Walbrook, though by this time, the river was no longer visible having been paved over due to pollution at the end of the 1400s. The house was the last building on the south side of Bucklersbury and must have been of considerable size having a chapel, a gallery, great hall, stables and a courtyard. It was here that Erasmus, the Dutch scholar and humanist stayed as More's guest. Herbalists and apothecaries traded in the area which was famous for its pungent smells. Shakespeare makes reference, in 'The Merry Wives of Windsor' to a 'smell like Bucklersbury'. By the late 1600s, it was known for tea, fans, cosmetics and fancy goods and was a popular shopping place favoured by Queen Mary, joint monarch with William III.

Four churches once stood in this area at the eastern end of Queen Victoria Street, two to the west of Bucklersbury. At the north end of Sise Lane stood the strangely named St Benet Sherehog, originally dedicated to St Osyth, a Saxon martyr. The name 'Sise' is a corruption of Osyth. John Stow relates how in the reign of King Edward III, the church was rebuilt by a local fishmonger, Benedict Shorne, hence its name. The tiny garden churchyard remained until it disappeared under the buildings of No. 1, Poultry in the mid 1990s. St Benet's together with the nearby St Pancras Soper Lane were both casualties in 1666. A third church,

A traffic jam outside *The Times* offices at the west end of Queen Victoria Street c. 1918. This part of the street was then largely occupied by manufacturing businesses – Richmonds made gas stoves; Story and Triggs to the right of *The Times*, were cabinet makers. The church of St Andrew by the Wardrobe is visible on the right.

also burnt in the Fire, was St Mary Woolchurch Haw, named after a beam in the churchyard where wool was weighed until the 14th century, and which stood on the present site of the Mansion House. Tragically, the construction of Queen Victoria Street itself caused the demolition in 1875 of the fourth lost church, St Antholin's, Budge Row. Considered to be one of Wren's finest creations, its delicate, graceful spire had been sold off some years before, after it had been struck by lightning and deemed unsafe. Its uppermost 16ft (5m) were re-erected in the grounds of what was then a private house, now itself demolished, at Round Hill, Forest Hill in south London where the spire can still be seen today.

St Mary Aldermary still remains on the corner of Bow Lane, now hemmed in to a tiny corner created when the construction of Queen Victoria Street sliced through existing streets. It is probably the oldest of all the City's churches that were dedicated to St Mary, hence its name, and dates originally from the 11th century. Before 1666, there was an astonishing total of 14 St Marys within the City walls. Unusually, Wren rebuilt this St Mary's in the Gothic style of its medieval predecessor, probably due to the re-use of substantial parts of the old church. The tower was added in about 1701 and could be to Nicholas Hawksmoor's design. The church now stands as a rare and important example of 17th century Gothic revival.

A little further west, Bread Street Hill ran south to Thames Street as an extension of Bread Street. The line of the former was lost after World War II rebuilding. Here before 1666 stood St Nicholas Olave, a church particularly favoured by cheesemongers and fishmongers, and in whose churchyard stood five almshouses of the Ironmongers Company. St Nicholas is the patron saint of sailors, children and thieves and it is strange that two churches dedicated to the same saint stood in such close proximity to each other. Around the corner, St Nicholas Cole Abbey still survives. Fishmongers also worshipped and were buried here; the surrounding streets occupied by their trade – Old Fish Street and Friday Street, after the religious custom of eating fish on this day. In the 1500s, a wealthy fishmonger paid for Thames water to be brought to a large tank in Old Fish Street Hill, for the 'care and commodity' of fishmongers, presumably for washing in. The origins of the name 'Cole Abbey' are unknown; though it may be a corruption of 'coldharbour' – a medieval word meaning shelter. It is said that, after the construction of the District Line below the street outside, smoke from the then steam locomotives seeping through outlets from the tunnels so blackened the church that it became known as 'Cole Hole Abbey'.

The College of Arms on Queen Victoria Street, whose present building dates from 1670, originally had no major street to its north or south; to its west ran St Benet's Hill (now Godliman Street); to its east, St Peter's Hill. Founded in 1485 by King Richard III, it is now, as then, occupied by the Kings of Arms, Heralds and Pursuivants, who under the directorship of the Earl Marshal of England, the Duke of Norfolk, are responsible for great state occasions such as Coronations and State Openings of Parliament. They also have jurisdiction over all existing coats of arms and responsibility for granting and design of new ones.

Just to the west, and occupying the land between the present Queen Victoria Street and Knightrider Street from 1572, were the buildings known as Doctors' Commons. This was where doctors of civil law practised and the Ecclesiastical and Admiralty courts were held. Licences for quick marriages could also be obtained, the ceremonies taking place in the nearby church of St Benet, now to be found on the opposite side of Queen Victoria Street. Charles Dickens describes Doctors Commons as *A little out of the way place, where they administer what is called Ecclesiastical Law and play all sorts of tricks with obsolete old monsters of acts of Parliament, which three-fourths of the world know nothing about.*

Many cases were trivial and often lasted for years. Changes in legal practices in the 1850s led to relocation of the courts, some to the Royal Courts of Justice in the Strand, and the fact that it was no longer in use led to its demolition in 1867 to make way for Queen Victoria Street.

The large 1860s office building on the north side of the street at No. 146 has an open bible carved in stone over the entrance, with the inscription 'The Word of the Lord endureth for ever'. It was designed as the headquarters of the British and Foreign Bible Society, founded in 1804, to 'encourage circulation of the Holy Scriptures' and distribute them throughout the world. The warehouse to the rear held half a million bibles.

Next door stands the curiously named church of St Andrew-by-the-Wardrobe. Revealed only when Queen Victoria Street cut through its churchyard, it was originally hidden amongst tiny alleyways. The King's Wardrobe stood to the north of the church from the 1360s when the house of nobleman John Beauchamp was requisitioned by the monarchy as a store for clothes, armour, coronation robes, beds, tapestries, robes of the Knights of the Garter, etc., and existed until the Great Fire.

The church of St Andrew was originally known in the 1200s as St Andre del Castillo, in reference to its close proximity to two 11th century Norman castles

Looking east along Queen Victoria Street in about 1910. The building in the distance, to the left of the Royal Exchange portico, was demolished in the mid 1920s and replaced by Sir Edwin Cooper's National Provincial Bank (now NatWest). Shops on the left include William Poore, stove manufacturers, and stationers Partridge & Cooper.

built as defensive fortifications on the western edge of the City. Baynard's Castle first stood near the present Blackfriars Lane but was rebuilt in 1275 on a river-side site south of the church and east of the entrance to Puddle Dock. In 1428, a new castle, then very much a royal residence, was built here by Henry V's brother, Duke Humphrey, creator of the first royal palace at Greenwich. The second castle, Montfichet, stood to the north of the church and was very small – a fortified tower rather than a castle – and was in ruins by the early 1200s.

To the west side of St Andrew's church ran Puddle Dock Hill (now St Andrew's Hill). West of this street and south of Ireland Yard, was the site known as Printing House Square, named after the King's Printing Office which had been established here in the 1620s producing, by patent, bibles, prayer books and Acts of Parliament. In 1785, John Walters established the *Daily Universal Register* here, which three years later became known as *The Times*. The business expanded beyond the old premises, enveloping the neighbouring alleys and buildings until in 1874 a vast new building was built and not replaced until the 1960s. *The Times* finally moved from here to Gray's Inn Road in 1974. The last page of the paper had once stated 'printed and published in the Parish of St Andrew by the Wardrobe with St Ann Blackfriars in the City of London.

For 300 years from the late 1200s, this area was occupied by the vast complex of buildings which made up the Blackfriars monastery. Its land reached from the present St Andrew's Hill as far west as the River Fleet (now New Bridge Street) and almost as far as Ludgate Hill to the north. The Dominican monks, in their black habits, had been granted the land occupied by Montfichet and the first Baynard's Castle and in 1290, the heart of Eleanor of Castile, her body entombed in Westminster Abbey, was buried here. King Henry VIII's case for divorce against Catherine of Aragon was heard here in 1529 but eight years later, the monastery was closed as part of the King's dissolution schemes.

In 1578 the Blackfriars Playhouse was established in the monks' old refectory, and was initially used by companies of boy actors, and later taken over by Richard Burbage, Shakespeare (who owned a house in nearby Ireland Yard) and other actors. The Playhouse was closed down in 1642, at the outbreak of Civil War.

At the western corner of Queen Victoria Street opposite Blackfriars Station, a tiny pub, the Black Friar, stands in isolation – the only building surviving in this area from the beginnings of the street in the 1870s. Remodelled in around 1905, its ornate interior with decorative friezes showing monks drinking, fishing and sleeping, makes this the best example of an Arts & Crafts style pub in London.

SMITHFIELD

An 1811 view of the market area looking south towards St Paul's, showing livestock pens.

Until the construction of the Victorian cast-iron and glass meat market in 1867, West Smithfield was simply a vast open area, originally outside the City walls. (There never was an East Smithfield in this area – the street of that name lies just north-east of the Tower of London, on the eastern side of the City.)

In this space which was first known as the Smoothfield, a livestock market had been held since the 12th century. William Fitzstephen writes at this time of 'a smoothfield where every Friday there is a celebrated rendezvous of fine horses to be sold and in another quarter are placed vendibles of the peasant, swine with their deep flanks and cows and oxen of great bulk'. Smithfield was a live meat market; slaughtered meat was sold in Newgate Market further south.

From the 1220s, Smithfield became a City Liberty – outside the City walls but under its jurisdiction. So, as at Holborn and Temple Bar, Smithfield Barrs were built on the northern side of the space, at the south end of St John Street. Streets appropriately called Chick Lane and Cow Lane ran into the market from the west.

The hospital and priory church of St Bartholomew the Great were founded by the monk Rahere in 1123 and still occupy the site on Smithfield's south side over 850 years later. On the orders of Henry VIII, the priory was closed in the

1500s, but he allowed the hospital to continue its work and therefore a statue of the king graces the hospital's 1704 entrance gatehouse. Protestations of parishioners saved the quire of the church from destruction after the priory was closed and it remains today as London's oldest parish church. The church is reached from Smithfield through a 16th century timber built gatehouse which was hidden from view until a later façade which covered it was destroyed by a Zeppelin attack in 1916.

Cloth Fair runs along the north side of the church and takes its name from an important cloth market, St Bartholomew's Fair, held over three days in August from the 1100s. A public holiday for Londoners and attracting European cloth merchants, it was opened by the Lord Mayor by the cutting a of piece of cloth – the origin of the custom of ribbon-cutting to open events or buildings. One of Cloth Fair's pubs is called the Hand and Shears.

By the 1600s, the fair had deteriorated into a riotous affair with sideshows, entertainers, bull and bearbaiting, described by Ben Jonson in his play of 1614. Victorian disapproval led to its final demise in the 1850s and Londoners lost their oldest public holiday – Bank Holidays were not introduced until 1871. Built through priory land in the 1590s, the narrow street contains a 17th century four-storey merchant's house at No. 41-42 and, until the mid 20th century, houses also existed on the south side obscuring the church from view.

Jousting tournaments were once held at Smithfield, John Stow describes how 'knights well-armed and mounted' rode from the Tower. To the south, Giltspur Street was perhaps linked to the manufacture of gilded spurs.

In 1381 a crowd of men from Kent led by Wat Tyler, having marched on London, gathered in Smithfield as part of the Peasant's Revolt against the poll tax. Fourteen-year old King Richard II rode to meet them and hear their grievances. The uprising was eventually quelled after a skirmish resulted in Lord Mayor Walworth stabbing Tyler, who was subsequently beheaded.

Space outside the confines of the walled City was required for public executions and Smithfield was used for this purpose for almost three centuries. Scottish patriot William Wallace was put to death here in 1305 and during the reign of Mary Tudor in the 16th century, 200 Protestants were burned at the stake.

The live meat market continued to expand until, by the mid 19th century, chaotic conditions led to demands for its closure. Drovers bringing cattle from all over Britain often stampeded herds into the market and newspapers carried stories of people being trampled and gored in surrounding streets. Dickens vividly described the market in Oliver Twist: *the ground was covered nearly ankle deep in mire, and a thick steam perpetually rising from the reeking bodies of the cattle ... the whistling of drovers, the barking of dogs, the bellowing and plunging of beasts ... the crowding, pushing, driving, beating, whooping and yelling, the hideous and discordant din ...*

The live meat market closed in June 1855 and moved to Islington. Work began on the present buildings, Sir Horace Jones' grand structure – 631ft (192m) long and 246ft (75m) wide – which occupies the area where animal pens had previously been situated. Vast excavations created a four acre subterranean railway with hydraulic lifts to the market which was opened in 1867 by the Lord Mayor, when 1200 guests dined on boar's head and beef.

Cloth Fair looking towards the narrow entrance into Smithfield. On the left is the north door of St Bartholomew's church and a row of 17th century houses, now demolished, behind which lies the churchyard which today is visible from this viewpoint.

THAMES STREET

Known before the late 19th century simply as Thames Street, there is now a divide into Upper and Lower just west of London Bridge. The character of the area was always dominated by the river and its industries. Until the mid 20th century, wharves and warehouses lined the street especially to the south, intersected by yards and alleys leading to the Thames shore. Before the 1st century, today's street would actually have been under water.

The Thames of Roman London was a much wider and shallower waterway, the wooden waterfront of its port running just north of the line of today's street. By the 2nd century, the quayside had moved a little further south as land reclamation continued, and by the 3rd century lay along the line of the present street with wooden storehouses and shops built out into the river to a distance of 500ft (150m).

Near to the corner of St Mary at Hill, stood a grand house dating from towards the end of Roman occupation in the early 5th century, with under-floor heating and its own private baths. Public baths built between 70 and 90AD stood much further to the west at the south end of Huggin Hill, on a steep natural slope on the riverside.

A riverside wall was eventually built in the late 3rd century, to protect the City from invaders sailing upstream. As the centuries passed, the wall became destroyed by the force of the river and by the 11th century had ceased to exist. Gradually then, for the next 300 years, the city developed to the south, between Thames Street and the river. Today's riverfront lies more than 320ft (100m) further south than it had done in the early Roman city.

86

After the end of Roman occupation, the City was not resettled until the late 800s when it became re-established as a major port during the reign of Alfred the Great. Three landing places date from this time: Billingsgate, Dowgate and the earliest, Queenhithe, the shape of the inlet still clearly visible off the river today. Its name originating from the Saxon 'hyth' or dock, it is first mentioned in 899 as Aetheredeshyth. Later, during the early 1100s, it was renamed after Queen Matilda, wife of Henry I who took over collection of dues from the dock, a right to which other early queens succeeded.

From the late 1200s, the main point for collection and administration of customs duties and taxes was always located at the eastern end of Thames Street where the first Custom House was built. Geoffrey Chaucer was employed as Comptroller of Customs for the Port of London in the 14th century, and it was from here throughout the centuries that taxes were levied on items as diverse as coal, wig powder and on the number of windows in a house. Wren built a new Custom House after the Great Fire, which lasted only until 1714 when an explosion in an adjacent gunpowder store meant that it had to be replaced again. One hundred years later, yet another fire meant another rebuild, which was completed in 1828 creating an impressive 500ft (152m) façade along the river.

In 1559, the Legal Quays had been set up along this part of the Thames to handle all cargoes on which duty was to be paid, though by the late 18th century severe overcrowding of the river and the warehouses led to the establishment of the enclosed docks to the east. A wharf at Billingsgate has existed since the early 11th century and was always particularly connected with the import of fish. In the 12th century this became the main area within the City for eating houses supplying takeaway food: 'victuals of all kinds, baked, fried, or boiled'.[1]

For centuries, Billingsgate market operated in wooden sheds and small warehouses until in 1877, the grand new premises designed by Horace Jones, the City Architect, opened for business. Throughout the 19th and 20th centuries trading led to huge daily congestion outside the market as hundreds of fish porters congregated in Lower Thames Street, wearing their distinctive flat topped hats of wood and leather enabling them to balance high stacks of fish baskets on their heads. Billingsgate Market was also important for coal, much brought from the northeast of England. In 1770, the first Coal Exchange opened on the opposite side of Thames Street on the eastern corner of St Mary at Hill. It was replaced by a magnificent new Exchange, opened by Prince Albert in 1849. Incorporating a high circular tower, its intricately designed interior boasted a glass domed rotunda with wrought iron balconies and inlaid wooden floor. Road widening schemes in the 1960s led to its demolition; the private Roman bath-house mentioned earlier was found on this site.

At the south end of St Mary at Hill, the Hall of the Watermen and Lightermen has stood since 1780 though originally the company was housed just to the east of present day Cannon Street Station. They were founded in the late 1580s in order to regulate the thousands of men who had for centuries earned their living by carrying goods (the lightermen) and passengers (the watermen) on the river and to offer apprenticeships to those wishing to learn the trade, a role continued to the present day.

[1] William Fitzstephen.

The north side of Lower Thames Street in 1901. A group of children with a baby carriage stand outside No. 117 next door to the pub, which appears to have closed as the exterior is covered in posters. The narrow street is lined with wholesalers connected with the Coal Exchange visible in the distance, and with nearby Billingsgate Market.

Pudding Lane, a little further west, was home in the 1660s to the baker Thomas Farynor, the King's Baker. His shop, ten houses up from Thames Street, was where in the early hours of 2nd September 1666, what became known as the Great Fire began. The circumstances are unknown as Farynor stated later that the bread ovens were extinguished and checked at 10.00pm. At first the fire spread slowly but, moving west in the direction of Fish Street Hill, and south towards the river, soon engulfed the old timber dwellings and warehouses full of inflammable goods such as oil, brandy, tallow and hemp.

Before the Fire, eleven churches stood in Thames Street and one of the first to be destroyed was St Magnus the Martyr, at that time standing beside the approach to London Bridge, which until 1831 was situated slightly further downstream to the east. Henry Yevele, the architect of the nave of Westminster Abbey, was buried here in 1400. He owned a fine house in the area as did his contemporary, Hugh Herland, the King's carpenter, responsible for the oak hammerbeam roof of Westminster Hall. Next to the pre-Fire church, a waterwheel stood under the first arch of London Bridge, lifting water from the river and supplying Fish Street Hill and Gracechurch Street with a water supply. The new church, rebuilt by Wren, incorporated an archway under the Tower through which pedestrians accessed the bridge.

The hall of the Worshipful Company of Fishmongers standing appropriately beside the river, is their third home, rebuilt in 1834 after the construction of the new London Bridge. They were founded in the 1400s, and for about a hundred years were divided into stock fishmongers (dried fish) and salt fishmongers (wet fish), who were constantly in dispute. The steep-roofed Tudor wharfside building, which has been likened to a Venetian merchant's house, had a river entrance for goods with principal rooms, such as the Great Hall, situated on the first floor. However it was relatively close to Pudding Lane, and lost in 1666, though quick thinking saved most of the company's treasures which were thrown into a barge as the fire caught hold. During World War I, the Great Hall was used as a military hospital. Straw was laid on the road outside to deaden the noise of the passing carts and carriages.

In the years after the Fire, this area, where Upper Thames Street now begins, was regenerated with many fine houses. As early as 1668, Samuel Pepys took a walk along Thames Street and remarked, 'there I do see a brave street likely to be, many brave houses being built'. Two such houses survive in Lawrence Pountney Lane to the north, while on Lawrence Pountney Hill, a house built in 1703 for Thomas Denning, a salter, is the finest example of an early 18th century house in the City, perhaps in London.

The area to the south of Upper Thames Street, now occupied by part of Cannon Street Station (1866) was, from the 1260s, the London base for a group of merchants from German and Baltic cities, known as the Hanseatic League. They held valuable monopolies on goods such as hemp, linen, timber and grain and through power and wealth were able to negotiate many privileges and immunities. Their large complex of buildings included a fine hall, residencies and warehouses with their own river frontage where they led an insular existence using their own currency and consuming only German wines. It was known as The Steelyard, a 'steel' being a beam that was used for weighing imported goods. Their monopoly and preferential rights were withdrawn in 1598 by Queen Elizabeth I.

To the east of the station site, All Hallows Lane is named after the two medieval churches, All Hallows-the-Great and the-Less, which stood on Thames Street. All-Hallows-the-Less was lost in the Great Fire, but the 'Great' survived for a further two centuries, when, because its tower jutted out so far into the street that the wheels of passing carts scraped it as they struggled to pass by, the church was demolished to allow for the widening of the road. The land was sold to the City Brewery and a map of 1886 shows the whole site south to the river as occupied by its mash-house, malt-crushing plants, and fermenting vats. It was demolished in the early 1920s.

Whittington Garden today divides Upper Thames Street from College Street and the church of St Michael Paternoster Royal. Here in the pre-Fire church, Richard (Dick) Whittington, prosperous merchant, Lord Mayor and City benefactor was buried, having financed its rebuilding in 1409. His house was to the north of the church where with money left in his will, a college for priests was founded with a duty to pray for his soul and those of this family. Prior to this College Hill was known as Tower Royal; a tiny section of this street can be found to the north (see CANNON STREET). Endowments from Whittington's will also helped pay for the roof on the first Guildhall, the founding of Guildhall Library and rather oddly, the creation of a riverside public lavatory to the south of the church, flushed by the tide, which provided sixty-four places in two facing rows and was known as the Long House.

The 'Royal' in the church's dedication is a corruption of La Riole, a part of Burgundy, as this part of the riverside area, known as the Vintry, was particularly associated with the importation of wine. The Vintners' Company have been based on the south of the street since 1446 and still occupy their post-Fire hall of 1671, though it was re-faced in the early 20th century. Opposite the hall on the corner of College Hill, which then extended further south to Thames Street, stood St Martin Vintry church lost in 1666, though St James Garlickhythe a little further west was rebuilt. Every July, after the election of a new Master, the Vintners' Company walk to the church in procession, led by a man with a broom who sweeps Upper Thames Street, recalling past centuries when the state of the street would have made this necessary. The dedication 'Garlickhythe' reflects the area's connection with spice imports and from 1742 to 1903, Keen's Mustard factory stood just north-east of the church, giving its name to the expression 'to be as keen as mustard'. Before World War II, the spacious area which now

All Hallows the Great in an engraving of 1829. The church stood on the south side of Thames Street just to the east of today's Cannon Street station. The tower, which caused an obstruction to traffic, was demolished in 1876 and rebuilt to the south of the church. The church was then demolished in 1894 leaving the new tower which survived until World War Two.

surrounds the church was full of offices and warehouses connected with the fur trade (see CANNON STREET).

During the late 1860s and early 1870s, at the time when Queen Victoria Street and the District Line were constructed, many streets and alleys leading north from Upper Thames Street were re-aligned and re-named. Two churches in this vicinity were also demolished during this period, the Church authorities having been given the power to do so by Act of Parliament, and to sell the sites in order to finance the building of more places of worship in the suburbs. St Michael Queenhithe stood between Little Trinity Lane and Huggin Hill while on the eastern corner of Lambeth Hill stood St Mary Somerset. Thanks to the efforts of Ewan Christian, architect to the Church Commissioners, the tower was spared and still stands, surmounted with pinnacles and obelisks as a fine example of Wren's work. The church's name may be a corruption of Somers Hythe and before its demolition, stood not on Lambeth Hill but on Old Fish Street Hill, part of which still exists slightly further to the north. An 18th century map shows a lane to the west of the church curiously called Labour in Vain Hill.

A little further west lay Paul's Wharf where Portland stone transported from Dorset for the building of Wren's St Paul's Cathedral was unloaded. In the reign of Elizabeth I, her principal minister and advisor, Lord Burleigh, had a large house here. The wharf gave its name to two churches – St Peter Paul's Wharf, situated at the south end of St Peter's Hill was lost in the Great Fire; St Benet Paul's Wharf, where fourteen years before the Fire, the architect Inigo Jones was buried, has been London's Welsh church since 1879. First mentioned in 1111, today's tiny red brick post-Fire church is probably the work of Robert Hooke, City surveyor and Wren's collaborator in much of the City's rebuilding. All of the area around St Benet's was devastated by bombing on the night of 10th May 1941, the same night that the House of Commons was destroyed.

The character of the riverside wharf areas that had survived for centuries was swept away during World War II and subsequent road developments in the 1960s. Some small lanes survive but nothing like the numbers of earlier times when a maze of alleys, yards and passageways criss-crossed the land to the south of Thames Street between London Bridge and Puddle Dock. From the 19th century, vast warehouses dominated the district grouped together along the river with names such as Wheatsheaf Wharf, Crown and Horseshoe Wharf, Anchor and Albion Wharves, and interspersed with manufacturing and processing plants, large and small. Some streets led to the water's edge and some to dead end yards: Emperor's Head Alley, Black Raven Alley, Three Cranes Hill, Friars Alley, Brewers Lane.

The Fire Insurance map of 1886 shows the western area of Upper Thames Street housing granaries, iron foundries, kilns, cement storage, copperworks, paper merchants, crushing mills, warehouses for gum, spice, tea, coffee and cocoa, oil, paint, rope and twine, printers and manufacturers of stoves and glass. Dock workers, porters, hauliers, wharfingers, watermen and lightermen slaked their thirst in countless pubs with nautical names – The Steam Packet, The Yarmouth Arms, The King's Head and Mermaid to name but a few. Hundreds of horse-drawn vehicles crammed the then fairly narrow thoroughfare causing unimaginable traffic chaos as goods and cargoes were collected and off-loaded.

Opposite Billingsgate market at 7 o'clock one morning in February 1937. Traders' carts completely block the road outside the King's Head and Mermaid pub on the right. The viaduct carrying the approach road to London Bridge can be seen in the distance and to its left, the church of St Magnus the Martyr.

THREADNEEDLE STREET

George Sampson's 1734 Bank of England with the first of Robert Taylor's low level extensions of 1760 to the east. To the left is the church of St Christopher-le-Stocks demolished in the 1780s to make way for further expansion. St Bartholomew-by-the-Exchange to the right was demolished in 1841.

Unlike many City streets the origins of Threadneedle Street's name are unknown. It may be named after an old trading sign of Three Needles or somehow be associated with the livery company of Merchant Taylors, makers of tents and linen garments worn under armour, who have occupied premises on the south side of the street since 1347. Although much of their building was destroyed in 1666 and again 1940, some important parts survived including the library with its collection of rare books and portraits.

In 1243 on the south side of the street, on the corner of Broad Street, a hospital and church dedicated to St Anthony was founded on the site of a former synagogue. In the usual role of a medieval hospital, it assisted travellers, provided lodgings and gave help to the poor. This area of the street was often nicknamed Pig St, an animal associated with St Anthony, numbers of which apparently ran loose in street. In the 15th century, a school for boys between seven and twelve was founded here. Considered to be one of the finest grammar schools in London, it was also one of the 'free schools'. Classes ran from six in the morning until six in the evening. French Huguenots took over the school in 1550 but it was not rebuilt after 1666. On the same site in 1842 a grand Hall of Commerce was constructed. Paid for by a Mr Moxhay, biscuit maker, it was designed to rival the Royal Exchange, Lloyds and the Baltic, but became a bank in the 1850s and was demolished 20 years later.

None of Threadneedle Street's churches now survive – all having been demolished to make way for other building schemes. St Bartholomew-by-the-Exchange and St Benet Fink were demolished in 1841 to make way for the present Royal Exchange. The remains of Miles Coverdale, translator of the Bible into English, who was buried in St Bartholomew's in 1568, were reinterred in St Magnus the Martyr in Lower Thames Street. St Benet Fink was probably named after a benefactor called Finch (Finch Lane stands near the site) and here in 1801 the theologian Cardinal John Henry Newman was baptised. He was born in Old Broad Street nearby where his father, a banker, lived. St Christopher-le-Stocks had originally been built in the 1200s on the bank of the Walbrook River which ran roughly along the line of present day Princes Street. The church was dedicated to the patron saint of watermen, the second part of its name coming from its proximity to the Stocks Market, which then stood on the site of the Mansion House. Before 1666, the market sold meat and fish and afterwards, largely fruit and vegetables. When St Christopher's was demolished in the 1780s to make way for the Bank of England, an open space marking its churchyard was left within the confines of the Bank. It was here in 1798 that permission was given for the burial of a 6ft 7in (2m) 'giant' to protect his remains from body snatchers who had been offered large sums for procurement of the corpse.

The church of St Martin Outwich stood at the far eastern corner of the street (see BISHOPSGATE). Opposite, on the north side of Threadneedle Street, South Sea House was built in 1724–25. A huge edifice, four storeys high, with a grand central entrance portico, it was designed by James Gould. The South Sea Company had been set up in 1711 and had a monopoly on all trade with the Spanish colonies of South America and with the west coast of North America. Shares in the company became fashionable and desirable, especially when it agreed to take over the national debt in 1720, offering its company shares in exchange for government stocks. Speculation drove the price of shares ever higher, multiplying

South Sea House at the eastern end of Threadneedle Street. Built in the 1720s, it stood at the eastern end of the street on the site of present day Bank of Scotland (built 1903 for the British Linen Bank). South Sea House was demolished in 1902 having been occupied since the 1850s by the Baltic Exchange.

St Benet Fink shown here in 1811 was demolished in 1841 to make way for the third Royal Exchange. Wren's unusual church was ten-sided, its floor plan egg-shaped and with oval windows in the tower.

over eight times within a few months. Eventually confidence and prices collapsed, many were ruined and scandals emerged involving corrupt politicians – the South Sea Bubble had burst. The company itself, however, was basically an honest concern and continued trading until the 1850s. South Sea House then became the home of the Baltic Exchange until it was demolished in 1902.

The Baltic had begun life in Threadneedle Street in 1744 when the Maryland Coffee House changed its name to the Virginia and Baltick. Its customers were merchants, trading and negotiating transport of cargoes mainly with the American colonies and with the countries of the Baltic, from where tallow was a particularly important commodity. Threadneedle Street, like its neighbour, Cornhill, abounded in coffee houses in the 17th and 18th centuries – the Antwerp, the Antigallican, Grigsby's, and the African and Senegal.

In 1650, the first known 'job centre' was set up in the street by an enterprising and innovative merchant, Henry Robinson. There is no record of how long it survived, but he had high aspirations, advertising his venture as The Office of Addresses and Encounters 'where all people of each rank and quality may receive direction and advice for the most cheap and speedy way of attaining whatsoever they can lawfully desire' claiming that he would find employment for 'tutors, chaplains, butlers, barbers, cooks, nurses, dairymaids, masters of ships, gunners, surgeons, or common mariners' amongst many others.

In 1734, the Bank of England which had been founded 40 years earlier, moved into its first purpose-built home in Threadneedle Street. It had first bought the large house of the first governor, John Houblon, gradually then acquiring more surrounding land by buying up houses and taverns. This first building in the Classical style was enlarged in the 1760–80s by the addition of two wings by the architect Robert Taylor. He was succeeded by Sir John Soane, who remained as the Bank's architect for 45 years. Until this time, the bank was still surrounded by alleyways and small buildings but the construction of Soane's vast single storey building, completed in 1828, created the island site on which the Bank now stands. Today only the high outer screen wall of Soane's bank survives, though his design remained unaltered until the 1920s when the Bank was redeveloped and expanded to the plans of architect Herbert Baker. During building works two late 2nd century Roman mosaic pavements were uncovered, seen as evidence of high quality houses which then occupied the banks of the Walbrook stream. It was whilst working here as the Bank's Secretary in 1908 that Kenneth Grahame wrote Wind in the Willows. He had begun his career in the Bank as a gentleman clerk in 1876.

Until 1973, the perimeter of the Bank was patrolled overnight by a detachment of footguards – the Bank Piquet – and even in the 1950s, they still marched here each evening from either Chelsea or the Wellington Barracks near Buckingham Palace.

Threadneedle Street is the centre of this 1910 view of the Bank of England (left of picture) and the Royal Exchange. All of Sir John Soane's building except for the perimeter wall was destroyed in the 1930s when Sir Herbert Baker reconstructed and enlarged the Bank.

BIBLIOGRAPHY

Chronicles of London – Andrew Saint & Gillian Darley – (Weidenfeld & Nicolson 1994)

Walks in Old London – Peter Jackson (Collins & Brown 1993)

London Encyclopaedia – Ben Weinreb & Christopher Hibbert (Macmillan 1983)

In Search of London – H. V. Morton – (Methuen 1951)

The Moving Pageant – Rick Allen – (Routledge 1998)

London Before the Blitz – Richard Trench – (Weidenfeld & Nicholson 1989)

The Buildings of England London 1: The City of London – Simon Bradley & Nikolas Pevsner (Yale University Press 2002)

Vanished Churches of the City of London – Gordon Huelin (Guildhall Library Publications 1996)

The Changing Metropolis – Gavin Stamp (Harmondsworth 1986)

London Rebuilt – Harold P. Clunn (John Murray 1927)

London Marches On – Harold P. Clunn (Caen Press 1947)

The Oxford Book of London – edited by Paul Bailey – (Oxford University Press 1995)

London, The City – Claud Golding – (Robert Hale 1951)

A Traveller's History of London – Richard Tames – (The Windrush Press 1992)

Square Mile Walks – Belinda Morse – (Historical Publications 1989)

Heart of the City – Peter Rowsome – (Museum of London Archaeology Service 2000)

Wates Book of London Churchyards – Harvey Hackman – (Collins 1981)

Roman London – Jenny Hall & Ralph Merrifield – (HMSO/Museum of London 1986)

Eighteenth Century London – Nicola Johnson (HMSO/Museum of London 1991)

Fleet Street, Holborn & the Inns of Court – Roger Hudson (Haggerston Press 1995)

Street Names of London – Gillian Bebbington (Batsford 1972)

Victorian & Edwardian City of London From Old Photographs – James l. Howgego (Batsford 1977)

The Life of Thomas More – Peter Ackroyd (Vintage 1999)

Samuel Pepys: The Unequalled Self – Claire Tomlin (Viking 2002)

A Tour of Through London About the Year 1725 – Daniel Defoe (Benjamin Bloom 1929)

A Survey of London – John Stow (Reprint of 1603 edition: Dent 1980)

A Survey of London – John Strype 1720 (Printed A. Churchill, London 1720)

Inns and Taverns of Old London – Henry Shelley (Pitman 1909)

Boyle's View of London and Its Environs – Peter Boyle – (Published by Boyle 1799)

The Streets of London – John Thomas Smith (Richard Bentley 1861)

New View of London – Edward Hatton (R. Chiswell, A & J Churchill 1708)

The World of London – John Fisher Murray (Richard Bentley 1853)

MAPS

Copperplate Map of London c.1559

Ogilvy & Morgan – City of London Map 1676

John Leake – An exact survey of streets, lanes and churches comprehended within the ruins of the City of London – 1723

John Rocque's Map 1747

Noyce – City of London Map 1864

Goad Fire Insurance Maps 1886 and 1922

GW Bacon – New Large Scale Ordnance Atlas of London 1888

A to Z of Elizabethan London – compiled by Adrian Proctor and Robert Taylor (London Topographical Society 1979)

A to Z of Victorian London – George W. Bacon 1830-1922 (Lympne Castle: H Margery in association with Guildhall Library 1987)